Banking Operations

6th edition

Colin Watson BA, FCIBS,
Chartered Banker

GLOBAL
professional
publishing

Published in 2014 by
Global Professional Publishing Ltd

Global Professional Publishing Ltd
Random Acres
Slip Mill Lane
Hawkhurst
Cranbrook
Kent TN18 5AD
Email: publishing@gppbooks.com

ISBN 978-1-909170-11-7

Printed by

About the author

COLIN WATSON

Colin has over 30 years training design, delivery and management experience in the financial services industry. He has worked on numerous projects for most of the major banks on design, learning and development, business development, sales training, team building, project management, and leadership.

He has authored 14 study texts for banking institutes both in the UK and South-East Asia. These titles include Business Lending, Retail Banking, Risk Management and Managing People. In addition, Colin has held Chief Examiner posts with the Chartered Banker Institute for a range of subjects, including Specialised Lending, Call Centre Management and Strategic Management. He has also worked with the Institute of Financial Services University College on their Work-Based Learning and Advanced Credit Diploma courses.

Colin is a Fellow of the Chartered Banker Institute and a graduate of the Open University

Chartered Banker
Leading financial professionalism

The Chartered Banker Institute is the only remaining professional banking institute in the UK. The Institute has driven an agenda of customer-focused ethical professionalism throughout its history. It promotes professional standards for bankers, provides professional and regulatory qualifications for retail, commercial and private bankers in the UK and overseas, and offers professional membership to qualified individuals. The Institute is the only body in the world able to confer the status of Chartered Banker to suitably qualified individuals.

The Institute has taken the lead in the creation of major initiative to improve the professional standards of the sector in the UK. In 2011 the Chartered Banker: Professional Standards Board [CB:PSB] was formally launched supported by nine of the UK's leading retail banks and an Independent Advisory Panel. At the same time the Framework for Professional Standards was published together with the Chartered Banker Code of Professional Conduct.

To support its ethos of supporting professionalism in practice, the Institute works very closely with banks, other education providers and professional bodies to accredit relevant workplace or formal learning. Wherever possible the intention is to build clear routes from these programmes and qualifications into the Institute's own qualification and membership structure to encourage many more professionals in the banking sector to aspire to the status of Chartered Banker.

As a Chartered, professional education body, and a registered charity, the Institute has a duty to work in the public interest. Aside for supporting the professional development and career aspirations of its students and members, the Institute is also engaged in the work to provide financial education within schools through its Financial Education Partnership.

More information can be obtained from the Institute's website: www.charteredbanker.com

Contents

PREFACE

This text gives the reader an insight to the ways in which retail banks operate in the 21st century.

The relationship between the banker and customer is one that is not always formalised in a written contract, but the legal cases that determine this are described at the start of the book, along with an overview of some of the directives and Sourcebooks issued by the Regulator.

The services that are offered by banks are described next, before the different classifications of customer – both personal and business – are discussed. Remaining on the theme of the customer, the operation of accounts is reviewed next, both the day to day operations and more complex matters, such as the procedures to be followed when a bank is notified of the death of a customer.

Although cheques are not used quite so much by personal customers, they are still an important method of money transmission, so the regulations regarding the processing of cheques, along with the role of banks regarding cheques are described in the next chapter. More recent developments in money transmission are then examined, including the use of plastic cards, internet and telephone banking.

The core business of banking is the taking of deposits from savers and lending these to borrowers. This important function of lending is outlined in the next chapter, along with a discussion of lending products and the Consumer Credit Act.

The text concludes with an examination of securities for advances. When a banker lends to a borrower, repayment is never guaranteed as circumstances may prevail that prevent the borrower from repaying some or even all of the advance. Banks will often seek to mitigate this risk by asking the borrower to pledge an asset to the bank, so that if repayment is not forthcoming, the bank then has the option of selling this asset and so repaying the loan. The attributes of a good security, along with an examination of the types of asset that may be pledged as security are discussed in this chapter.

1 Banker/Customer Relationships

Objectives

By the end of this chapter, you should be able to:

- Explain what the functions of a bank are.

- Define what is meant by a bank customer.

- Outline the banker/customer relationship.

- Describe the purpose and content of the Banking Conduct of Business Sourcebook and the Lending Code.

Introduction

In this chapter we will start by discussing what a bank is. You will see that this is a more difficult task than might appear at first, although some statutes can help us. We will then move on to consider when a person becomes a bank customer and reference will be made to the relevant case law for guidance here. The next topic is the banker/customer relationship when we will examine the duties of both the banker and the customer. The chapter concludes with overviews of the Banking Conduct of Business Sourcebook, the Lending Code and the Treating Customers Fairly initiative – you may be familiar with these through your current employment.

What is a bank?

This may have seemed like a simple question to answer on the surface, but more difficult once your tried to commit your thoughts to paper! We all know what a bank is: an organisation that borrows money from one group of people and then lends the money to another group of people. So, that's a bank, or is it possibly also a building society or a credit union? Both of these types of institutions also borrow from their depositors and then lend the money borrowed to other customers. What therefore is the difference between a bank and a building society or a credit union? What is the difference between a bank like the RBS Group and Sainsbury's bank?

We must also consider the other services provided by a bank. Not everyone who uses the services of a bank deposits money with them, or borrows money from them. Perhaps the question is not so simple after all? It may come as a surprise to learn that the best legal minds have found it difficult to arrive at a definition which covers all the business activities transacted by a bank.

You may wonder why it is important that it is clear what type of business is a bank and which is not; after all, everyone has a rough idea of the type of business that is carried on by a "bank". As you study this book, you will come across situations where "banks" are provided with protection in certain circumstances. For example, when we look at cheques, you will discover that a bank obtains certain protection when it is dealing with a customer. It is therefore important to know what exactly a bank is and what a customer is.

Some Acts of Parliament, called statutes, have made reference to the main activities and features of a bank. Some definitions are more useful than others. The *Bills of Exchange Act 1882*, which is a very important statute in relation to cheques, states that a "banker" includes a body of persons who carry on the business of banking!

The definitions provided in some court cases do not take us much further forward. For example, one case determined that a bank is an organisation whose main business consists of the receipt of money on deposit repayable on demand by cheque. This definition is rather outdated and focuses on the provision of a current account which is only part of the business of banking. The definition does not cover all of the activities or the full range of services provided by a bank.

By now it is becoming clear that what at first glance appeared to be a very simple question is not really such an easy question to answer. Prior to April 1979, the definition of banking was neither precise nor final, but it was widely accepted that a person or establishment could not come within the definition of a bank unless the principal, or at least a substantial part of the business, consisted of receiving money for credit of a current account which the depositor might withdraw on demand by cheque.

The *Banking Act 1979* introduced a formal system of supervision of "banking" and prohibits any person – with certain exceptions – from accepting deposits in the course of carrying on a business. The Act also introduced the terms "recognised bank" and "licensed deposit taker" to make a distinction between institutions and the range of services they provided. It also set a minimum capital requirement for banks of £5 million and £1 million for licensed deposit takers.

The *Banking Act 1987* gave further powers of authorisation and regulation to the Bank of England but changed the definition of "recognised bank" and "licensed institution" to one of "authorised institution". This was further changed when the *Bank of England Act*, 1998 was introduced, transferring the powers of authorisation and regulation of UK banks to the Financial Services Authority (FSA) – which has now been superseded by the Financial Conduct Authority and the Prudential Regulation Authority. The *Financial Services and Markets Act 2000* strengthened the powers of the FSA even further.

With a few exceptions, it is illegal to accept deposits from the public unless authorisation has been obtained from the Prudential Regulation Authority (PRA). This authorisation is called "Part 4A Permission". The vetting procedures are stringent and are designed to ensure that consumers are protected from unscrupulous individuals setting themselves up as deposit takers. Details of these "authorised institutions" are maintained by the PRA.

What is a customer?

Having struggled to arrive at a satisfactory definition of a bank, hopefully we will have an easier job in defining a customer. Again we can look to decisions in court cases – case law – to point us in the right direction. One case determined that the term "customer" implied a course of dealing or a habit of calling at the bank from time to time; another that some sort of account must be maintained.

This seems straightforward enough, but what about someone who has just opened an account with the bank? How often must this person call at the bank before being classed a customer? It would seem obvious that as soon as someone has opened an account with a bank, he or she immediately becomes a customer.

Case studies

This view was confirmed in the case of Ladbroke and Company -v- Todd, 1914 (which is considered in the section on cheques) the judgement of which decreed that the relationship of banker and customer begins as soon as an account is opened and the first cheque is paid in and accepted by the banker for collection and not merely when the cheque has been paid.

In Great Western Railway Co -v - London and County Banking Co, 1901 it was held that a person is not a customer unless he has some sort of an account, either a deposit or current account or some similar relation with the bank.

In Taxation Commissioners -v- English, Scottish and Australian Bank, 1920, it was held that a person becomes a customer as soon as he opens an account.

In the case of Woods -v- Martins Bank, 1959, it was held that a person could become a customer even before he had opened an account, if it was his intention to open one and he subsequently did so.

Woods -v- Martin's Bank, 1959

The plaintiff, Woods, a young man without business experience, was considering an investment in Brocks Refrigeration Ltd, a private company banking with a branch of the defendant bank. He sought the advice of the branch manager and was told that the investment would be a wise one, the company being financially sound. Acting on this advice he invested £5,000 in the company and subsequently, having opened an account at the same branch, invested further funds on the manager's advice.

Unknown to the plaintiff, the company's account was heavily overdrawn throughout this period and the branch manager was under considerable pressure from the District Head Office to have the debt reduced. Eventually, the plaintiff lost nearly £16,000 and brought an action against the bank and the manager for fraud or negligence.

It was held that the manager's advice was grossly negligent but not fraudulent. The bank was liable for the negligent advice given and its plea that it was no part of its business to give investment advice was rejected after examination of its advertisements.

The plaintiff had become a customer of the bank from the time the instructions to make the first investment had been accepted although the current account was not opened until nearly one month later.

The banker/customer relationship is deemed to begin:

As regards an account holder

- as soon as the bank opens an account for someone (with the intention that the relationship be permanent). In the case of the Great Western Railway Co -v- London and County Bank Co Ltd it was held that the cashing of cheques over a long period of time for a person who had no account with the bank did not make him a customer.

As regards any other banking service

- as soon as the bank agrees to provide that service (for example advice on investments as in Woods -v- Martins Bank).

The relationship between banker and customer

Early thinking on the relationship between a bank and its customer was that a banker was a custodian of the customer's funds. This type of thinking implies, however, that the customer will receive the same notes and coins as they paid in initially and if correct, would restrict the banker's ability to deal with the customer's funds and to onlend funds to other customers. If you think about it, this is a fundamental function of a bank. In very basic terms, banks act as a link between those members of society who have excess funds – savers – and those who have a shortfall of funds – borrowers. The technical term for this is "financial intermediation". We will return to this theme of financial intermediation later on in the text.

It was eventually agreed that the basic relationship between a banker and customer was that of debtor and creditor. In the case of Royal Bank of Scotland -v- Skinner 1931, it was held that the banker is not merely the custodian of money, as when money is paid in it is used by the bank for the purposes of its business and that the bank undertakes an obligation to repay an equivalent amount.

The relationship between banker and customer is one of contact – although when an account is opened, there is usually no written contract apart from the account opening document. In the next chapter we'll look in detail at the relationships that exist between a bank and its customers as customers take advantage of the many services offered by a bank.

The banker's duties

When we looked at the definition of a bank, it was apparent that the main business of banking in the legally defined sense is the receipt of money withdrawable by cheque. It follows from this that the bank's principal duty is to honour customers' cheques on demand.

The bank must honour its customers' cheques provided that:

- there are sufficient available funds in the account of the customer who has issued the cheque

- the cheque is technically in order (that is, it has been signed, the amount in figures is the same as the amount in words, etc)

- there is no legal or other impediment preventing the banker from making payment.

Bankers would therefore be in breach of their basic duties to customers if they wrongfully dishonoured cheques. It is therefore the duty of the banker to ascertain beyond any doubt that a customer has insufficient funds before refusing payment of a cheque or returning a cheque unpaid. You will be aware that the use of cheques has been severely curtailed over the past decade. However, the principles outlined above still hold true.

Another duty of the banker is that of secrecy which is an important feature of the banker's relationship with the customer. A bank must not disclose any details of its dealings with a customer, even after the customer no longer maintains an account with the bank. The duty of secrecy applies just as much to an account in the name of an individual vis-à-vis his or her spouse as with any other account. If a banker were therefore faced with a request from a customer to be advised of the balance on her husband's account, the request should be politely declined; otherwise the bank could be liable to the husband in an action for damages.

There are four circumstances when a bank is permitted, and in some cases compelled, to divulge information concerning its customers' affairs. The circumstances which impinged on a banker's duty of confidentiality were set out in the judgement in the case of Tournier -v- National Provincial and Union Bank of England, 1924 and are:

1 where disclosure is under compulsion by law

2 where there is a duty to the public to disclose

3 where it is in the interests of the bank to disclose information

4 where the disclosure is made with the consent of the customer.

■ Disclosure under compulsion of law

The exemption under compulsion by law may be divided into three headings:

- disclosure under compulsion of a court order

- disclosure to an official who is statutorily entitled to compel disclosure

- disclosure where there is an onus on the bank to disclose information.

The first category includes the *Bankers Books Evidence Act 1879*. An order under this Act is probably the most familiar example of disclosure under compulsion by law. The Act was not designed to enforce bankers to give evidence before the courts but to deal with the form in which evidence may be given and to avoid the inconvenience of a bank being deprived of its books during court cases.

Orders under the Act are usually given by the relevant court, and although they empower the pursuer or defender to take copies of the relevant entries in the bank's books, in practice the bank will provide the copies and certify them in terms of the docquet contained in the Act.

A party to legal proceedings can apply to court for leave to inspect and take copies of entries in a banker's books for the purposes of such proceedings. This power applies to an account of a person (or a company) who is also party to the litigation or that of a person closely connected with the litigation. This provision applies to both civil and criminal proceedings, although it has largely been superseded by more recent statutes with regard to criminal investigations.

The power applies to entries in a banker's books (which includes records of the customer's transactions, details of cheques, etc) but does not extend to correspondence between the bank and its customer, nor to paid cheques and paying-in slips retained by the bank after the conclusion of any transaction.

■ Duty to the public to disclose

In the Tournier case it was said that many instances of such a duty might be given, but the judges did not actually give any, except to refer to another case "where dangers to the State or public duty may supersede the duty of agent to principal". Thus, where in a time of war the customer's dealings indicated trade with the enemy, a duty to disclose could arise.

However, there is no duty to give information to the police about a customer suspected of a crime, but the bank cannot plead in this way if the end result is to conceal fraud. It has been established that the police must show they have a real interest in the account, and are not just trawling for information which may or may not help them.

■ **Where it is in the interests of the bank to disclose**

Where there is court action between the bank and its customer some disclosure about the customer's affairs will be necessary.

Where a customer has given their express consent, there can obviously not be a breach of secrecy, but this authority should be in writing. For instance, a customer may authorise the bank to provide his accountant with banking details in order to assist the accountant to complete accounts.

■ **Where disclosure is made with the consent of the customer**

Until the major banks introduced a new status enquiry system with effect from 28 March 1994, it had been a long held view that when a customer entered into a banker/customer relationship with a bank, the banker had the customer's implied authority to respond to enquiries about the customer's status and financial standing provided the enquiry was received from another banker or certain trade protection societies or other organisations. It was not the practice to respond directly to individuals or businesses.

The new system introduced certain procedural changes. Individuals or businesses wishing to obtain a banker's opinion now send their request direct to the bank concerned. That bank responds direct to the enquirer rather than channel the reply through the enquirer's bankers. However, reliance is no longer placed on the implied authority of the customer to respond to status enquiries and the bank will only reply to an enquiry with the express consent of the customer who is the subject of the enquiry.

You may have encountered this situation where, for example, you have obtained credit from a finance company, say to assist with the purchase of a car, and they wish to obtain an opinion from your bank.

The banking industry introduced model forms of combined enquiry and consent forms and most banks now charge the enquirer for providing this service. People who submit status enquiries can either pay by means of plastic card or by cheque.

If the enquirer does not understand the reply to his status enquiry, he is free to ask his own bank to express a view as to the meaning of the response, that is through experience and knowledge of how the responses are framed; a bank can usually decode the message.

The customer's duties

The customer owes certain duties to the bank. The customer should ensure that when cheques are issued there are sufficient funds in the account, or at least a suitable overdraft has been arranged in advance to enable the cheques to be paid when presented to the bank. If a bank pays a cheque on which the signature of the customer is forged, it will be unable to debit the customer's account.

Similarly, if a cheque has been altered and the alteration has not been authenticated by the customer, then in some circumstances the bank will not be able to debit the customer's account. The customer has a duty, however, to ensure that cheques are issued in a manner which does not facilitate alteration and that, in the event of the customer becoming aware that his signature is being forged on cheques, he must take all steps that are open to him to minimise the bank's loss.

Examples could include:

- not leaving any spaces between words when writing the amount of the cheque

- drawing a line between the last word and the amount box

- when inserting the figures in the amount box, using a long line between the "pounds" and "pence" figures in order to use the full width of the box.

The judgements in two court cases, which are looked at in more detail in the chapter on cheques, confirm the position.

The Banking Conduct of Business Sourcebook (BCOBS)

The Banking Conduct of Business Sourcebook (BCOBS) sets out the rules and guidelines by which the FCA regulates retail banking. The Sourcebook provides guidance on financial promotions and communications with banking customers throughout the lifetime of their relationship with a bank. It specifies how and when communications should be entered into with customers depending on the type of account held and what the information being provided relates to; for example, pre-notification of charges, etc.

BCOBS also covers changes to the charging structure, interest rates and terms and conditions of an account, as well as a number of other areas previously covered by the Banking Code.

The BCOBS came in along with the Payment Services Directive (Europe-wide regulation of payment service providers) and the Lending Code.

Case studies

In the case of London Joint Stock Bank -v- Macmillan and Arthur, 1918 it was held that if a customer is careless in the manner in which he draws a cheque, and fraudulent alteration of the cheque is facilitated, then it is the customer and not the bank that should bear any loss.

In the case of Greenwood -v- Martins Bank Limited, 1931 a customer was aware that his wife was forging his signature on cheques that were being paid by the bank. The customer did not inform the bank until after his wife had died and then attempted to sue the bank for recovery of the sums paid away. His action was not successful.

The Lending Code

The Lending Code is a self-regulatory code which sets minimum standards of good lending practice when dealing with:

- Consumers

- Small businesses employing fewer than 10 people and with a turnover of less than €2M

- Charities with an annual income of under £1M

The Code covers:

- Loans

- Credit cards

- Charge cards

- Current account overdrafts

The Code does not apply to merchant services, non-business borrowing secured on land, or to sales finance.

Compliance with the Code is monitored independently and is enforced by the Lending Standards Board.

The Key Commitments

Subscribers to the Lending Code will act fairly and reasonably in all their dealings with customers by, as a minimum, meeting all the commitments and standards in the Code.

The key commitments are:

- Subscribers will make sure that advertising and promotional literature is fair, clear and not misleading and that customers are given clear information about products and services.

- Customers will be given clear information about products and services before, during and after the point of sale, including how they work, their terms and conditions and the interest rates and charges that apply to them.

- Regular statements will be made available to customers (if appropriate). Customers will also be informed about changes to the interest rates, charges or terms and conditions.

- Subscribers will lend money responsibly.

- Subscribers will deal quickly and sympathetically with things that go wrong and act sympathetically and positively when considering a customer's financial difficulties.

- Personal information will be treated as private and confidential, and subscribers will provide secure and reliable banking and payment systems.

- Subscribers will make sure their staff are trained to put this Code into practice.

Areas covered by the Code

The areas covered by the Lending Code are:

- Communications and Financial Promotions

- Credit Reference Agencies

- Credit Assessment

- Current Account Overdrafts

- Credit Cards

- Loans

- Terms and Conditions

- Financial Difficulties

- Complaints

- Monitoring

Treating Customers Fairly (TCF)

Fundamentally, the concept of TCF is that banks should carry out their business in a way that ensures that the customer gets fair treatment. However, before looking at what TCF is, it is worthwhile considering what TCF is not.

Firstly, TCF is *not* about creating a satisfied customer – the customer may be unhappy about a decision by the bank not to grant them credit facilities, but the customer may well have been fairly treated.

Secondly, TCF is *not* about each bank providing an identical level of service – all banks are different and have different levels of resources, so they will go about providing their customer service in their own way.

Lastly, TCF is *not* about taking customers' decision-making powers away from them, nor is it about removing the responsibility for decision making away from the customer. What banks are expected to do is ensure that customers have enough information to make an informed and educated decision.

The Financial Conduct Authority has provided examples of both good and bad TCF, but it has not dictated how TCF should be applied in a bank – rather it is up to each bank to make this decision. What the FCA has done is identify behavioural drivers which are likely to have a significant effect on whether or not a bank will meet the requirements of TCF.

These behavioural drivers are:

- **Leadership**

  Senior management should provide middle management with sufficient direction and ensure that adequate controls are in place to monitor. A bank's business plan should provide the ongoing development of policies, management information and procedures.

- **Strategy**

  TCF should be incorporated into any changes that are made to the business. For example, a bank's mission statement could state that the bank will treat its customers fairly. Also procedures could be put in place to ensure that all of the changes implemented by the bank have had an earlier analysis of TCF, such as when designing a new complaints procedure, or implementing new documentation. It would be expected that before a change is delivered, whoever in the bank has responsibility for the final sign-off of this change should ensure that TCF requirements have been embedded.

■ **Decision making and challenge**

The bank should encourage staff to challenge anything they see which contradicts TCF. This could involve the establishment of focus groups to review both new and existing processes and procedures to question and challenge how they meet TCF expectations. Banks should communicate to their staff that each individual has the responsibility of ensuring that TCF is being considered in everything that the bank does. Such an approach will ensure that a TCF culture is embedded throughout a bank.

■ **Controls**

Banks should identify, interpret and use relevant management information which will allow them to monitor TCF effectively and show that the bank is indeed treating its customers fairly. Relevant management information could include customer surveys, mystery shopper results, complaints returns and so on. Any issues or concerns that come out of this management information should be investigated fully and any necessary actions taken.

This type of information could also be used by a bank to demonstrate that they are complying with TCF. For example, customers could make an increasing number of enquiries about how long it should take for a cheque to clear and, as a result, the bank may include a clearing timetable on its website.

■ **Performance management**

Staff should receive performance management objectives that demonstrate what TCF means for the particular role carried out by that member of staff, both in terms of what they should do (their actions) and the way they should do this (their behaviours).

■ **Reward**

- Controls: Firms should identify, collect, interpret and use relevant management information to monitor TCF effectively and to demonstrate that they are treating customers fairly.

Banks should consider how targets can be met while still treating the customer fairly. This requirement will guard against the likelihood of a member of staff treating a customer unfairly simply to achieve a performance management objective; for example, selling a customer a credit card that they had no need of in order for the member of staff to reach a sales target.

The FCA has also defined six customer outcomes that they expect banks to demonstrate that they have achieved:

- Customers can be confident that they are dealing with a bank where the fair treatment of customers is central to the corporate culture, therefore a bank should ensure that TCF is incorporated into the business plan and strategic plan. Policies and procedures should reflect TCF and the concept of TCF should be present in staff training. As discussed earlier, management information that relates to TCF should be scrutinised and appropriate corrective action taken.

- Products and services marketed and sold in the retail market should be designed to meet the needs of identified customer groups and should be targeted accordingly. Therefore all products must include the needs of TCF before they are signed off and offered by the bank to its customers.

- Customers should be provided with clear information and kept appropriately informed before, during and after the point of sale. Banks should ensure that all customer documentation adheres to TCF; for example, plain English should be used throughout.

- Where customers receive advice, the advice is suitable and takes account of their circumstances.

- Customers are provided with products that perform as the bank has led them to expect and that the associated service is of an acceptable standard and as they have been led to believe.

- Customers do not face unreasonable post-sale barriers imposed by banks to change product, switch providers, submit a claim or make a complaint. Adhering to Retail Banking Conduct of Business Standards will help banks be compliant here as well as adherence to other codes and guidelines.

Compliance with TCF will be monitored and regulated as part of the FCAs routine assessments.

Question   1

Go to question section starting on page 243

Check with the answer at the back of the book.

Review

Now consider the main learning points which were introduced in this chapter.

Go through them and tick each one when you are happy that you fully understand each point.

Then check back to the objectives at the beginning of the chapter and match them to the learning points.

Reread any section you are unsure of before moving on.

It is difficult to define precisely what is meant by a "bank". The Banking Act 1979 introduced a formal system of supervision of "banking" and prohibits any person from accepting deposits in the course of carrying on a business. The Act also introduced the terms "recognised bank" and "licensed deposit taker" to make a distinction between institutions and the range of services they provided.

☐

While there is no statutory definition of a bank, with a few exceptions, it is illegal to accept deposits from the public unless authorisation has been obtained from the PRA.

☐

As soon as someone has opened an account with a bank, they immediately become a customer. However, it has also been held that a person could become a customer even before opening an account, if it was their intention to open one and subsequently did so.

☐

The relationship between banker and customer is one of contract.

☐

The bank's principal duty is to honour customers' cheques on demand.

☐

Another duty of the banker is that of secrecy. There are four exceptions: when disclosure may be permitted under compulsion of law, where there is a duty to the public to disclose, where it is in the interests of the bank to disclose information, or where the disclosure is made with the customer's consent.

☐

A duty of the customer is to ensure that when cheques are issued there are sufficient available funds in the account. The customer also has a duty to ensure that cheques are issued in a manner which does not facilitate alteration and that, in the event of becoming aware that their signature is being forged on cheques, they must take all steps to minimise the bank's loss.

☐

The Banking Conduct of Business Sourcebook sets out the rules by which the FCA regulates retail banking.

☐

The Lending Code is a self-regulatory Code which sets out the minimum standards of good practice when lending to individuals, small businesses and small charities.

☐

Treating Customers Fairly is an initiative that requires banks to ensure the fair treatment of customers in all aspects of banking services.

☐

Key words in this chapter are given below. There is space to write your own revision notes and to add any other words or phrases that you want to remember.

Part 4A Permission

Treating Customers Fairly (TCF)

Bills of Exchange Act 1882

Financial Services and Markets Act 2000

Bankers Books Evidence Act 1879

banker's duties

customer's duties

Banking Conduct of Business Sourcebook

Lending Code

Multiple choice questions   **1**

Try these self-test questions to assess your understanding of what you have read in this chapter.

The answers are at the back of the book.

1   The Bills of Exchange Act 1882 is important in relation to which one of the following types of banking services?

  A   bill payments

  B   cheques

  C   direct debits

  D   foreign exchange services

2   Which one of the following pieces of legislation prohibits a non-excepted person or organisation from accepting deposits in the course of carrying out a business?

  A   Financial Services Act 1986

  B   Building Societies Act 1997

  C   Banking Act 1979

  D   Bills of Exchange Act 1882

3   The authority given by the PRA to persons seeking to set up a bank is called:

  A   Part 4A Permission

  B   A Certificate of Incorporation

  C   PRA Authorisation

  D   A Banking Certificate

Multiple choice questions   **1**

4 In the context of disclosing information that would otherwise be confidential, which one of the following statements is true?

A   a bank always requires the consent of the individual concerned to disclose confidential information

B   a bank may disclose if it is in the interests of the customer concerned

C   a bank need not disclose information on a customer unless a court order has been made to this effect

D   a bank may disclose confidential information if it is in the public interest to do so

5 The relationship between a depositor and a banker is one of:

A   trustee and beneficiary

B   member and depositor

C   debtor and creditor

D   bailor and bailee

6 Legally, the relationship between a banker and its customer is which one of the following?

A   membership

B   contract

C   custodian

D   trustee

Multiple choice questions   **1**

7 What would be the consequence of a bank disclosing the balance on Susan's account, held in her sole name, to Freddie, her husband?

   A   the bank would be prosecuted

   B   the bank would be deregistered under the Data Protection Act 1998

   C   Susan may be awarded damages against the bank

   D   there would be no consequence to the bank as Susan and Freddie are legally married

8 Which one of the following is NOT covered by the Lending Code?

   A   A charge card

   B   A credit card

   C   An overdraft

   D   Sales finance

2   An Outline of Bank Services

Objectives

By the end of this chapter, you should be able to:

- Explain the operation of savings and investment accounts.

- Describe basic lending facilities offered by banks.

- Outline money transmission and payment services.

- Describe the share dealing and investment advice services of banks.

- Explain what is meant by trustee and executry business.

- Differentiate between insurance and assurance.

- State the travel facilities bank customers use.

- Describe the safe custody services banks offer to customers.

Introduction

In the last chapter we looked at definitions of a bank and a customer and the various relationships that exist between them. We considered the most basic of banker and customer relationships. Now we will look at some of the range of services that a bank can offer to its customers, particularly:

- savings and investment accounts

- lending facilities

- money transmission

- payment services

- share dealing and investment advice

- executor and trustee services

- insurance and assurance

- travel facilities

- safe custody services.

Savings and investment accounts

One function of a bank is to attract depositors of funds. Banks pay interest on many of the funds deposited with them, and this business is profitable for banks as they can on-lend some of the funds deposited with them to other customers at a higher rate of interest. If a bank does not have sufficient deposits to fund its lending, it may have to borrow on the money markets which is much more expensive than paying interest to depositors. If a bank has surplus deposits which it does not need immediately to fund lending, these funds can be placed on the money market at a rate of interest which will be higher than the rate of interest which it will pay to its depositors. There is great competition for deposits between individual banks and between banks and building societies and other organisations; for example, online businesses that offer fund management services.

The rates of interest paid by banks will vary depending on a number of factors. Some types of accounts will offer different rates of interest depending on the balance maintained in the account.

The motivation that people have to save and invest may be very similar – what differentiates the saver from the investor is their underlying attitude. Saving involves no risk to the capital that has been set aside by the saver. You will be aware of the government scheme which offers savers a degree of protection for savings should the organisation they have deposited funds with run into financial difficulty. Normally, the saver will have the expectation that this capital will grow with the addition of interest added to the original sum. Normally savings are the surplus funds that people set aside, either for a specific purpose, for example, a holiday, or as a contingency for a "rainy day".

On the other hand, investment carries the risk of loss of some or all of the capital. The higher this level of risk, the greater the potential return the investor could hope to make. Not surprisingly, investment returns usually outperform savings returns in the medium to long term.

A further way that we can differentiate savings from investments is the way in which the return is made. Savings pay interest, whereas investment returns are based on a number of factors, such as capital growth and dividends payable to shareholders. Examples of investments would be buying stocks and shares which will either provide income by way of dividends or growth as the share price of the shares increases. Purchasing property can be regarded as an investment as property values are generally expected to rise as time goes on. However, property prices can fall as well as rise, and those considering investment in property should be made aware of this.

Competition between the banks themselves and between banks, building societies and other institutions is fierce and each bank will attempt to offer a range of savings and investment accounts which will cater for all of their customers' requirements.

We will shortly look at a typical range of savings and investment accounts which can be offered by banks. In addition to considering the types of account shown here, look at the range of savings and investment accounts offered by your own bank or organisation and consider the relative features of each. Remember, generally speaking, the rate of interest will increase with the amount deposited and the length of time for which the funds will be committed, and lower interest is usually the compromise for convenience and instant access.

Current accounts

The current account is a traditional type of account which has been offered by banks for many years. In the early days of banking, before banks offered such a wide range of savings products, most banks only offered a current account and some form of deposit account. A current account provides the customer with a high level of convenience and is very popular with personal customers although it is perhaps more popular with business customers who will often have a substantial number of transactions going through their accounts. These accounts are sometimes referred to as money transmission accounts, as they are used to deposit and withdraw funds, usually on a frequent basis. We will look in more detail at money transmission later in this chapter.

Funds can easily be deposited into a current account and withdrawn just as easily. There is no minimum sum required to open an account and there are no limits on the amount that can be deposited or withdrawn at any time. Traditionally, funds were withdrawn from a current account by means of a cheque drawn by the customer either payable to him/herself or payable to a third party. We will look at cheques in some detail later, but for now we can see that a major benefit of a current account is that it provides customers with a useful means of settling bills and accounts and allows the customer to go shopping, pay bills, purchase petrol, pay for holidays and large household or electrical items without having to carry large quantities of cash. It is also possible to make automated payments from a current account by way of standing orders and direct debits, faster payments, plastic card, mobile phone, or by using the bank's telephone centre or website. We will look at all of these facilities later in this course.

Another feature of a current account is that it is possible to have an overdraft on the account, that is, it is possible to withdraw more funds than have been paid in, but it is essential for the customer to agree with the bank beforehand that it will be permissible for the account to become overdrawn and the maximum amount by which the account may be overdrawn – the overdraft limit. The simplest way to think about an overdraft is to consider it as the negative balance on a current account.

If cheques or other payment requests, such as standing orders or direct debits, are issued by the customer without funds being in the account to meet them when they are presented for payment, if an overdraft limit has not been authorised, or if the amount of the overdraft is or will be in excess of the limit, then the bank may return these items unpaid to the bank that has presented them for payment. Such a course of action will often cause considerable embarrassment to the customer and may well have an adverse effect on both their credit rating and the outcome of any future credit scores.

A number of larger retailers no longer accept cheques as a means of payment and will rather accept cash or a plastic card. When a plastic card is used, it is either swiped through an electronic reader by the retailer or, more commonly, the customer inserts the card into the reader and is prompted to key a four digit Personal Identification Number (PIN) into a keypad. The transaction is then authorised electronically and the relevant receipts are produced. We will return to this theme in Chapter 6 when we examine Plastic and Electronic Banking.

In the event of a current account becoming overdrawn, the customer pays interest to the bank at an agreed rate over the bank's reference rate. In addition, if the account is overdrawn without a limit being agreed beforehand or if the limit is exceeded, the rate of interest payable on any unauthorised overdraft or any excess may well be much higher than the rate of interest for authorised overdrafts.

In the UK, the rate of interest charged by the bank is linked to the Bank of England Base Rate which is reviewed monthly by the Bank of England's Monetary Policy Committee. You will no doubt have heard and read in the media about the movements in this rate and the rationale behind them.

Example

Assume that the Bank of England Base Rate is currently set at 6% and your bank's reference rate shadows this. If a customer has an overdraft agreed with your bank at 4% above reference rate, then this facility will incur a rate of interest of 10% (6% plus 4%). Should Bank of England Base Rate be reduced to 5%, your bank's reference rate will follow suit and so the interest charged on this overdraft will now be reduced to 9% (5% plus 4%).

We will look at the factors which inform your bank's decision as to what margin above base rate they set the overdraft rate at in the chapter on lending. The interest charged on an overdraft is only applied to the outstanding balance of the account – not on the agreed overdraft limit, therefore, if you have an agreed overdraft limit with your bank of say, £1,000, but your account is only overdrawn by £657, then you only pay interest on this lower figure.

The main benefits of a current account are:

- ease of access

- a convenient method of payment

- security.

As a compromise for such benefits, customers are only paid a low rate of interest – or sometimes no interest at all – on funds deposited in current accounts. However, provided the account remains in credit, there is normally no service charge. If the account becomes overdrawn at any time during the period for which service charges are calculated, normally monthly, these charges are normally applied for the whole month – not just the period for which the account was overdrawn. We will look at service charges in more detail later relating to the operation of customer accounts.

Customers may receive regular statements from the bank or may view these online, detailing all the transactions on the current account and advising of the current balance. Some of the services offered on a current account are:

- cash withdrawal card

- standing orders

- direct debits

- faster payments service

- debit/payment card

- telephone banking

- internet banking.

Interest bearing current accounts

Traditionally banks did not pay interest on credit balances on a current account. Customers did not seem to mind as they enjoyed many other benefits from having this type of account, often holding two accounts with the same bank – a current account for organising day-to-day living and other expenses, and a deposit or savings account to which they could transfer surplus funds. For a long time therefore, banks could regard credit balances on current accounts as an interest-free loan to the bank which could be onlent to other customers, thus earning interest for the bank.

Eventually, as competition intensified, and particularly when building societies started offering bank-type accounts such as a cheque book account which was interest bearing, banks offered their customers interest paying current accounts. Given the convenience of current accounts and the fact that customers have instant access to their funds, the rate of interest payable will be among the lowest rates paid by the bank, although most interest rates are tiered so that the more that is held in the account, the better the rate of interest will be. Some banks attempt to gain a competitive advantage over their rivals by offering a higher rate of interest.

Basic accounts

As the name infers, these are accounts which offer the customer a basic range of money transmission facilities, with a plastic card for withdrawals of cash at an Automated Telling Machine (ATM). It is also possible to have automated payments credited to the account (such as for wages) and payments may also be made from the account by way of standing orders and direct debits. Overdrafts are not permitted on such an account.

High interest cheque accounts

This type of account is similar in some ways to a current account although the rate of interest paid is greater than the rate on interest paying current accounts. The customer will still have instant access to their funds, but there may be restrictions on the number of cheques that may be issued in a given period and cheques may require to be for not less than a stated amount, say £250 or 10% of the balance on the account. A minimum amount is also normally required to open the account, say £2,500, and it may be a condition that the balance on the account does not fall below a minimum sum, otherwise normal current account conditions will apply.

Savings accounts

These types of accounts are sometimes known as deposit accounts. The rate of interest paid on savings accounts is higher than the rate paid on interest paying current accounts, although normally if the customer is looking for a high rate of interest they will not be attracted to a savings account.

The main advantages of a savings account are:

- there is no minimum sum required to open the account nor minimum balance to be maintained

- the customer has instant access to the funds.

Savings accounts are therefore suitable for short term savings, such as for a holiday or household goods. Some customers may also be attracted to splitting their savings between two types of account, keeping some of their savings instantly available with any surplus being committed for a term at a higher rate of interest. One point the customer should bear in mind if pursuing this strategy is that the combined balance on the two accounts, if deposited in the one account, may result in a balance that passes the threshold to qualify for the next tier of interest above the rate currently being paid. Overdrafts are not permitted on savings accounts and the customer cannot issue cheques on the account.

Investment accounts

Customers with surplus funds which are not immediately required can earn the top rates of interest offered by banks by investing their funds in an investment type of account. A minimum amount is usually required to open the account and the customer may have to give notice of withdrawal, often as much as 90 days. Again the interest rates will be tiered with larger balances attracting higher rates of interest.

Whilst these accounts require the customer to give the appropriate period of notice, it might be possible for the customer to obtain instant access; however, there will be some form of interest penalty which the customer must forgo in order to obtain the instant access.

It is also possible for depositors to attract money market rates by investing the funds for a fixed term which could be as long as five years. The bank can pay money market rates as it will sometimes onlend the funds in the market for a similar term. For this reason it would not be possible for the customer to withdraw the funds during the term of the deposit. The rate of interest varies depending on the amount of the deposit and the term.

Individual savings accounts

An ISA is a tax-free savings account available in the UK.

- They can consist of cash or stocks and shares.

- There is no tax liability.

- There are maximum annual limits set for the amount that can be paid into an ISA. These are reviewed by the government annually. For the year 2011/2012, individuals are permitted to subscribe up to a maximum of £10,680 in an equity ISA. Up to £5,340 can be put into a cash ISA, with the balance of up to £5,340 being invested in the equity element.

- Stocks and shares ISAs can be taken out by anyone over 18 who is ordinarily resident in the UK for tax purposes. A cash ISA can be opened by anyone over 16 years who is ordinarily resident in the UK for tax purposes.

Financial Intermediation

As discussed earlier, banks have a key role to play in an economy as they act as a conduit between those in the economy with too much money (savers) and those who do not have enough (borrowers). Fortunately, the presence of banks in an economy means that the bank can make it easier for savers and borrowers to have their needs met.

When a bank lends money to borrowers, it needs to access these funds from another party. Whilst it is possible for a bank to borrow short-term from another bank on the inter-bank market, the bank can also use funds that are deposited by savers in order to fund the lending it makes available to borrowers.

A problem can be that most deposits made by customers are repayable on demand – around 70% in fact. However, when a bank lends funds to a borrower, the terms and conditions of this contract will state how repayment is to be made. Take a capital and interest mortgage as an example; this is a long-term loan that is normally repayable by monthly instalments. If we assume that the borrower adheres to the terms and conditions of their agreement, then the bank will only receive relatively small repayments of the loan on a monthly basis. However, there is a danger that savers will seek to withdraw their funds at any time.

The bank will know from past experience that not all savers will seek to withdraw their money all at the same time, therefore, it is safe to lend much of these funds out, secure in the knowledge that not all savers will withdraw their deposits immediately.

The bank will always have to take care that they have sufficient funds in their ATMs and branches to meet the withdrawal demands of customers and banks use sophisticated modelling techniques to forecast what their cash requirements are. Should there be any shortfall forecast, then the bank needs to have enough notice of this to make alternative arrangements – perhaps by borrowing funds from other banks.

The benefits of financial intermediation can be summarised under these headings:

Maturity Transformation: as discussed, deposits and loans will have different maturity dates – typically deposits are repayable on demand, whilst loans are repayable in the longer term. However, as banks are receiving deposits and making credit available to a wide number of customers, they are able to amalgamate these transactions. However, if banks did not exist, if an individual wished to borrow, they would need to find someone with excess funds who was happy to lend this money to them for the period that they wished to borrow for. This could pose problems, as many savers will want to be able to access their funds relatively easily if they need to and would not be attracted to lending their money to another person for (say) 25 years.

Amount Aggregation: in addition to the above point, borrowers would not only have to find someone willing to lend to them for an appropriate period, this person would also have to have the right amount of money available. Were this not the case, then the borrower would need to enter into a range of transactions where the total amount lent to them eventually was enough to meet their purposes. On the other hand, banks are able to take varying levels of deposits and combine these to make larger loans to some borrowers.

Risk Transformation: over the years, banks have become adept at assessing credit. In recent years, this has been developed further through the use of credit scoring systems. Again, very few individuals would have the knowledge or expertise what would allow them to make sound credit decisions, and as a result, when they lend their funds on to another party, they would have the increased risk of not getting their money back. This would make savers even less likely to lend their money to another party – especially to someone that they did not know.

Location Transformation: this is the final area to consider. A bank may obtain deposits from savers who live all over the country (and sometimes even all over the world). They are then able to use these funds to lend to borrowers who again can be geographically dispersed. Were this facility not available, it could prove difficult for borrowers to find suitable savers who did not live near them.

You can see from the above that if banks did not carry out this function of financial intermediation in an economy, then savers and borrowers would be in the difficult position of having to barter for money with the attendant problems described.

Lending facilities

As you have just seen, banks borrow funds from depositors which are then advanced to other customers. The margin between the rate of interest paid by the banks and the rate charged to borrowers is profit for the bank. You will appreciate therefore that lending is a very important part of a bank's business. We will look at the general principles of good lending later when we will also look at some of the lending products offered by banks. Here we will briefly summarise some of these products.

Overdrafts

You will recall that banks sometimes permit current account customers to issue cheques for sums in excess of the credit balance on the account. The customer is thus permitted to overdraw on the account and pays interest on the amount of the overdraft. Overdrafts are convenient for both personal customers who may need additional funds to tide them over until their salary is received and businesses that may require assistance from the bank to balance the timing of bills and expenses that require to be paid with receipts from customers and debtors.

Overdrafts are repayable on demand and are normally subject to annual review. Some financial service providers now automatically offer overdraft facilities on some current account products.

When a customer has an overdraft, it is expected that the account will swing from credit to debit; for example, for a personal customer, the account may show a debit balance prior to the monthly salary being lodged to the account, when it will swing into credit again.

For a business customer, the overdraft may be to help finance the purchase of stock. When the customer pays for this, it would be expected that the balance of the account would swing into debit, and once the stock is sold and funds are received, the account should swing back into credit. When an account remains in debit permanently, this is referred to as hard core borrowing.

Personal loans

Personal loans are normally granted for the purpose of consumer purchases such as cars, holidays, consumer durables such as televisions, fridge-freezers and for home improvements such as a new fitted kitchen, double glazing, the building of a conservatory, etc. Personal loans are not restricted to these purposes and may be granted for any purpose that is both legal and within the bank's Credit Policy.

Interest is charged on personal loans at a flat rate which means that it is calculated on the total amount of the loan for the full term and applied to the amount of the loan at the commencement of the repayment term. The total amount is then divided by the number of monthly instalments to determine the amount of the repayment instalments. Personal loans are not usually secured and the maximum term of a loan is normally ten years.

When a personal loan application is received, it is usually credit scored to determine whether or not the bank is willing to grant the facility. We will look at credit scoring in more detail later in the course.

House purchase loans

House purchase loans (normally referred to by customers as mortgages) were traditionally offered by building societies but are now offered by banks at rates of interest that are competitive with the building societies.

The amount available to borrowers will normally be a stipulated multiple of the customer's salary or a multiple of joint borrowers' combined salaries. We will look at house purchase loans in more detail later in the course.

Equity release or capital release loans

When we discuss "equity" in this context, we are talking about the difference between the market value of the property and the total value of the mortgage and any other borrowing secured on the property.

For example: if a house has a market value of £250,000 and a mortgage of £150,000, then the equity is £100,000 – i.e. £250,000, less £150,000 = £100,000.

There are a number of ways in which a bank may be willing to lend against this asset:

Conventional mortgage or remortgage

Here, the borrower makes an application to the bank (who have provided the original mortgage) to lend against the equity in their home. Using the figures above, we will assume that the bank is willing to lend up to 60% of the equity in the property.

It would be £60,000 – in other words, 60% of the equity, which is £100,000. This assumes that the borrower's financial circumstances confirm that they could afford to repay such a loan.

Second mortgage

In this case, the borrower seeks to borrow against the equity in their home – but with a different lender. This may not always be the best way forward for the borrower, as the lender would wish to take security over the property, by way of a second bond (or mortgage), and the borrower would need to pay the fees associated with this.

From the lender's point of view, they may feel that it would have made more sense for the borrower to approach the mortgage lender first. It may be assumed that the borrower did, in fact, do this and for some reason the mortgage lender has declined the deal. This would make the second potential lender cautious about proceeding.

Lifetime mortgage

This is a facility that is generally looked at by people aged 55 years and over. They are mostly taken out by people who have no borrowing on their property, but wish to raise some cash on the basis of the equity on their home. With such an arrangement, the amount that can be borrowed rarely exceeds 25% of the market value of the property. Normally, such a loan will not have a fixed repayment date – rather it will be repaid either on the death of the borrowers, or when the house is sold.

Home reversion plan

This final arrangement is not a loan at all – rather it is where all or part of the property is sold to a finance provider and the occupant then becomes a tenant for life, or until the property is sold. Such an arrangement could mean that the property owner is able to raise a larger cash sum than they could have under a lifetime mortgage, but the amount would still be expected to be significantly less than the market value of the property.

In the UK, these products are regulated under the Mortgage Conduct of Business (MCOB) rules and most second mortgages fall under the Consumer Credit Acts 1974 and 2006.

Money transmission and payment services

Money transmission is the transfer of money from one party to another, normally from the receiver of goods and services to the supplier of goods and services. The simplest form of money transmission is the physical transfer of cash from one party to another. Another basic form of money transmission is cheques which again are physically transferred either in person, for example in a shop or by post.

Money transmission is a central function in today's society as the transfer of value is involved in almost every aspect of everyday life. Firms need to transfer funds to suppliers for the goods and services required to conduct the firm's business. Firms also need labour which they have to pay for in the form of wages and salaries. Individuals are the recipients of wages and salaries which they in turn transfer to various parties. They will most likely transfer a significant proportion of the money they receive in respect of their home, whether to a landlord or to a bank or building society which advanced them funds to enable them to purchase their house.

Individuals also require basic commodities such as food and energy and will transfer their money to the providers of such commodities. The money transferred to the firms producing commodities can then be transferred to the suppliers of goods and services and the suppliers of labour (individuals) in return for the values provided by them and so it goes on.

There are a number of methods of money transmission other than cash or cheques and the banks provide a number of payment services, some of which are:

- standing orders

- direct debits

- faster payments service

- bank giro credits

- banker's drafts

- credit cards

- charge cards

- debit cards

- telephone banking

- internet services.

- mobile apps

We will take a further look at cash and cheques here and also consider the first five of the above – standing orders, direct debits, faster payments, bank giro credits and banker's drafts. The remaining payment services will be covered later when we deal with plastic cards and electronic banking.

Cash

In spite of the technological advances that have been made in recent years and the wide range of payment services available from banks, cash is still probably the most popular means of money transmission as far as individuals are concerned. Cash is easy to use and is a very convenient method of transferring value, especially in a series of relatively small transactions.

We are probably further away from a cashless society than you think. The UK Payments Council tells us that 61% of transactions are still made in cash – although these are for lower value transactions.

Traditionally individuals received their wages and salaries in the form of cash which provided them with an immediately available form of purchasing power. In more recent times there has been a move towards other methods of paying wages and salaries – the most common being by credit transfer straight into the employee's account.

If wages are paid directly into a bank account on which the use of a cheque book is permitted, the funds in the account can immediately be transferred to third parties by means of a cheque. In such circumstances individuals will still have a need for cash as, for example, it would not be practical to write a cheque for very small amounts and cash is still the only acceptable method of payment for things parking meters. Individuals will therefore wish to convert some of the money in their bank account into cash, which is usually done by withdrawing funds via an ATM, although it is possible to withdraw cash at the counter of a bank either with a plastic card or by signing the relevant withdrawal form. Most bank branches have ATMs and they are also increasingly available at locations other than banks such as shopping centres and other retail outlets, etc. Many retailers who accept payment by plastic card will also be happy to provide a "cash back" service to customers, whereby when a payment is made by card, the customer is able to have an additional amount added to the transaction, which they receive from the retailer by way of cash. Retailer can be happy to provide this service as it reduces the amount of cash that they hold on their premises and can also reduce their bank charges as if they pay less physical cash into their bank accounts, then the level of bank charges will be reduced accordingly.

The customer's plastic card has a magnetic strip and chip containing identifying features which will be picked up by the bank's main computer system when the card is inserted in an ATM. The customer's personal identification number (PIN) is conveyed to the bank every time the ATM is used. This is a security measure which prevents the card being used by anyone else. In some banks, cash withdrawals made at the counter may also be authorised by the customer keying their PIN into a keypad. It is also possible to use a card for a "touchless payments" – these are restricted to small amounts and rather than the customer having to key in their PIN, they simply touch their card against a sensor in the retailer's premises.

The main advantages of ATMs are that:

- they are available for use 24 hours a day, 7 days a week

- they are also very simple to operate – the customer is guided through the transaction by a series of on-screen instructions.

The additional features that may be available at an ATM include:

- accept deposits

- process a cheque book request

- send out marketing information

- print the customer's balance

- print a statement of the customer's last ten transactions

- pay bills

- change the customer's PIN

- transfer funds between different accounts

- top up a mobile phone.

- make a donation to specified charities

Cheques

Cheques play a vital role in banking operations. In a later chapter devoted entirely to them we will look closely at the definition of a cheque and the status of the various parties to a cheque. We will also look at the way in which a cheque is transferred from the bank at which it was lodged to the bank of the customer who actually issued the cheque. For now we'll consider the advantages and disadvantages of a cheque as a means of settling payments.

The main advantage of cheques is that they provide a safe and convenient method of transferring money. Cheques can be made out for any amount, therefore they can be used for settlement of large transactions and can also be sent by mail.

If a cheque were to fall into the wrong hands it would not normally be possible for the person then holding the cheque to obtain value for it and it would also be possible for the person who has issued the cheque to ask the bank not to pay the cheque if it is ever presented for payment.

However, if the drawer (or issuer) of the cheque has reason not to wish the cheque to be paid on presentation (for example, if it has gone missing in the post), it is possible to request that on presentation the bank refuses to pay the cheque. This is called stopping or countermanding the cheque. A bank will normally charge the customer for this service.

The time between a cheque being lodged at the bank of the person in whose favour the cheque has been drawn and the cheque being paid by the bank of the person who has issued the cheque is known as the time that it takes the cheque to clear. Some people will not wish to pass over their goods or services until they are in receipt of cleared funds. The time taken for cheques to clear is normally two or three business days, depending on whether the bank accounts of the person in whose favour the cheque has been issued and the person issuing the cheque are at the same branch of the bank or at the same or different banks.

An advantage of the clearing system as far as the person issuing the cheque is concerned is that there will be a delay of a number of days between the cheque being issued, the goods being received and the person's account being debited. This is more of an advantage if the cheque has been issued on an interest bearing current account.

Standing orders

A standing order is a signed authority given by a customer to a bank instructing the bank to make regular payments from the customer's account to a specified party at stated times for a stated period or until further notice. Standing orders are designed for fixed regular payments such as insurance premiums, council tax and loan repayments. A standing order is a safe and convenient method of transferring funds and avoids the need to remember to send payments every month or to send cash or cheques through the post, or to call into a bank to make a bank giro credit payment.

The customer signs a standing order mandate authorising the bank to debit their account and transfer the sum involved to the bank account of the third party. No further action is necessary by the customer and the bank account will be debited on the agreed date every month, week, quarter or annually, as the case may be.

If the account to be debited and the account to be credited are both held at the same branch of a bank, it should be relatively straightforward for the bank to make the transfer. The situation is a little more complicated if the beneficiary's bank account is with another bank. In such circumstances the bank will make use of VOCA. The banks are members of VOCA which handles all of the transfers between banks.

Direct debits

Direct debits are similar to standing orders in some ways, but there are several important differences. Direct debits are used for making regular payments and the transfers are handled by VOCA. They also require the written authority of the customer. The fundamental difference, however, is that rather than the customer's bank remitting the payment via VOCA, the beneficiary instigates the debit and advises the bank of the amount involved. The authority that the customer gives to the bank is to comply with instructions received from the beneficiary of the direct debit to debit the customer's account. Direct debits are more suitable than standing orders for payments for irregular amounts and are now more popular than standing orders as they do not need to be amended every time there is a change in the payment amount (such as a change in the mortgage interest rate).

Example

A customer may wish to pay their power bill automatically through their bank account which can be done either by standing order or direct debit. If the customer elects to pay by standing order, the actual amounts that will be due to the supplier of the power company will not be known at the outset as the amount will depend on the consumption of fuel. The customer and the power company agree an amount which is roughly in line with the customer's anticipated usage of fuel and the customer pays this sum by standing order. At regular intervals the amounts paid will be reconciled with the actual sum due and adjustments can be made. However, if the customer elects to pay by direct debit, as soon as the power company has taken a meter reading and has calculated the exact sum due to them, they could instigate a direct debit and take the correct sum due from the customer's account.

Direct debits are also useful for annual subscriptions, telephone bills, payment of television licence fee and numerous other purposes. The customer may cancel direct debits and in certain circumstances arrange to have payments recalled. That said, there is still some nervousness on the part of some customers to sign direct debit authorities as it is the payees who initiate payments. Some customers are understandably nervous that they will lose control of the amounts that are taken out of their bank accounts and many prefer standing orders for this reason. Banks, however, apply very strict controls on those organisations wishing to operate the direct debit system.

As an added protection to the customer, there is the Direct Debit Guarantee Scheme which protects customers who have direct debits set up on their accounts. Organisations that use direct debits are required to meet stringent legal, financial and administrative requirements. When they make an application to use direct debits, this must be supported by an authorised sponsor, such as their bank. The organisation must also sign a standard indemnity. Therefore, if a customer has had a payment made from their account by way of direct debit, this scheme will indemnify them against any loss or incorrect debit.

Faster Payments Service

Many banks now offer customers the Faster Payments service, by which it is possible to make automated payments that are guaranteed to reach the beneficiary's account within two hours, although in reality receipt is almost instantaneous. While banks have offered same-day payment services in the past (through the Clearing House Automated Payments System), these have been targeted at high-value transactions; for example, they are use in the settlement of house purchases and sales. Faster Payments, on the other hand, is targeted at smaller value transactions of up to £100,000 and can be used as a substitute for standing orders.

Bank giro credits

A bank giro credit is a credit transfer form used by customers for making non-automated payments to accounts domiciled at a branch or bank other than the branch where the customer's account is held.

The bank giro credit transfer slip is completed by the customer and contains details of:

- sorting code of the bank to which the funds are to be transferred

- name of the bank

- branch of the bank

- name of the account to be credited

- account number

- who is making the payment

- in some cases, an identifying reference, for example for a catalogue payment

- amount.

Many organisations, such as utility companies, telephone and internet providers and credit card companies issue statements and bills and include a preprinted bank giro credit as a tear-off portion of the bill or statement to make settlement easier for the customer who only has to sign and date the credit transfer and lodge it together with the required amount of money at the branch counter. The bank then sends the credit to the bank account of the party issuing the bill or statement.

Bank giro credits pass through the clearing system, therefore the funds will take longer to reach the beneficiary's account than would be the case if the funds had been sent electronically or by standing order or direct debit.

Banker's drafts

We have already discovered that the fact that a cheque has been issued doesn't guarantee that the person it has been issued to will be paid. The customer can place a stop on the cheque, or the bank can refuse to pay the cheque on the grounds that the customer did not have sufficient funds in the bank account, or the overdraft on the account was not sufficient to permit the cheque to be paid. This uncertainty can be removed if the supplier of goods or services is given a banker's draft as payment. Payment is guaranteed unless the draft has been lost or stolen and the payee doesn't have to wait until the funds have been cleared.

The use of banker's drafts has diminished in recent years, as large payments may be made by way of plastic card or by faster payments. In addition, settlements for large transactions, such as house purchase, is usually made by a CHAPS payment. We will look at these later in the course.

Share dealing services and advice

For many years, banks have provided a range of services and advice relating to investments in products not offered by them. The buying and selling of shares, government stocks and unit trust units, and local authority loans, can all be arranged. Banks may also offer investment advice and manage portfolios of investments through specialist departments and/or through subsidiaries.

The customer's written authority is relayed to a broker/dealer who buys or sells the shares according to the customer's instructions; for example, a minimum price may be stipulated rather than "at best". Shortly after a bargain has been struck, the customer will receive a contract note detailing the consideration (number of shares x share price), date of bargain, dealing charges, etc, and, normally within a fortnight or so, monies will be received or paid. It is now possible to receive this information online if the customer prefers.

Although they can be realised quickly if necessary, shares should be regarded as long term investments, as prices fluctuate from day to day, and they have to rise sufficiently to cover dealing costs as well as provide capital gain for the investor. You will be aware that in the autumn of 2007, concerns over the American sub-prime mortgage market caused large daily fluctuations on global stock markets.

Customers who opt for this method of investment are free to make their own decisions but may be exposed to too much risk if there aren't sufficient funds to spread the individual investments around different industries, sectors and markets. Monitoring of performance is also time consuming – there is a need to review progress on a daily basis, the financial press or internet must be reviewed and decisions have to be taken as to what to buy and sell, and when to do it.

Investment advice

A share dealing service is normally on an execution only basis, that is the customer has already decided to buy or sell shares and which shares are to be bought or sold. Some of a bank's customers may have surplus monies to invest but may not be sure how they wish the monies to be invested. Branch bankers are not specialist advisers in investment and would not wish to run the risk of being sued for negligence if, on the recommendation of a banker, a customer incurred significant losses on the stock exchange. Decisions on which shares to invest in should be left to the customer.

However, if the customer is looking for advice from the bank as to suitable investments, there are specialist departments to help the customer. It is important to establish whether the customer is looking for income or growth. If the former, they should look for an investment that will provide regular dividends or place funds in an investment account that pays interest monthly or quarterly. The bank account option will only be attractive of course in times of high interest rates. If the latter, then shares which are expected to rise in value will be more attractive than shares which merely provide good dividends.

It should be remembered that growth and income are not mutually exclusive in a company share. In fact, if a share pays good dividends it will be popular with investors, which is likely to drive up the share price. It is also important to discover if the customer has other considerations they would want to take into account when their portfolio is being built; for example, they may wish to avoid certain types of organisations, say in armaments, or those companies involved in animal testing.

Investment and portfolio management

Banks can offer a service, usually through a specialist subsidiary company, to customers who wish their investments to be completely managed by the bank. An investment strategy will be agreed which will take into account all of the customer's circumstances, including whether or not they have any strong beliefs on certain issues that will affect investment decisions as mentioned above.

Once the strategy has been agreed, day-to-day management of the portfolio is carried out by the bank company. The customer can either allow the bank discretion to purchase and sell shares on their behalf or the bank may be required to obtain their authorisation before making any changes to the portfolio.

Monitoring fluctuations in share values and switching funds between investments can be a time consuming business. The customer may therefore feel that this task would be better handled by full time staff with specialist knowledge of the market.

Executor and trustee services

Banks provide executor and trustee services, but as such services are highly specialised, involving detailed knowledge of the relevant law and taxation, they are provided by specialist departments of the bank. Before we can begin to understand these services, we must first understand the functions of an executor and a trustee.

An executor is someone who is appointed to ensure that the wishes of a deceased person, as set out in his or her will, are carried out. Normally an executor will be appointed in terms of the will itself, but if the person making the will has failed to nominate an executor, one can be appointed by the court. If the deceased died without making a will (intestate) an executor may be appointed by the court to wind up the deceased's estate.

A trustee is a person who has been trusted to hold and administer property or assets for the benefit of others. A trust can be created at any time by someone transferring assets, either cash, investments or property, into the name of a trustee and directing, in terms of a trust deed, that the trustee holds and invests the assets for the benefit of others, for example, the children of the person creating the trust, and that the trustee makes payments out of the trust fund to the beneficiaries at certain times.

Customers will sometimes have banks appointed as an executor or a trustee in preference to individuals, as an executor must be someone who is expected to live longer than the person making the will and similarly a trustee should live long enough and retain the faculties to see the trust purposes fulfilled. As a bank is an organisation with corporate personality, it will by definition live longer than the customer.

In addition, trusts often involve large sums of money and it is desirable that a trustee has financial acumen and specialist knowledge and is able to make tax-efficient decisions when investing the trust's funds. A bank's specialist department can provide all of these services. Another reason why a bank may be appointed as executor or trustee is that it is essential that the relevant duties are carried out in an impartial manner. The division of family property is often a cause of acrimony and there are obvious benefits in having affairs administered by a party which is some way removed from the beneficiaries.

Insurance and assurance

A number of banks have been associated with insurance and life assurance companies for many years, acting as agents for these companies. In the highly competitive financial market, relationships have changed as financial services organisations have actively promoted such services.

Insurance is the means by which an individual or business can obtain recompense, from the insurance company, in respect of loss or of damage to property, personal accident, loss of business profits, etc suffered by the insured. A premium is paid for the cover provided. Life assurance provides payment on the death of the insured but may also include payment on a specified date should the insured survive until that date.

The key difference is that assurance is concerned with certainty, insurance with possibility.

Currently, many banks provide insurance and assurance advice and products through branches as well as through specialist companies. These services are dependent on the extent of the particular organisation's involvement in this field. There are three possibilities:

- the organisation may act as insurance broker, that is, offer the customer a choice of insurance company

- the organisation may be a tied agent, that is, insurance/assurance is arranged through one company only

- the bank may sell their own products.

In the first two cases, the organisation earns a commission from the insurance company and life assurance is fairly lucrative. By acting as insurers, the organisation derives profit from the premiums.

Safe custody services

Probably the earliest banking service offered to the public was the acceptance of items of value for safe keeping. Today, title deeds, share certificates, life assurance policies, wills, jewellery, rare coins, etc may be lodged with many banks for safe keeping. Such items can be deposited in open envelopes, sealed packages or locked boxes, or safe deposit boxes or lockers may be available in some branches.

Unsealed envelopes are appropriate when the customer requires to deal with the contents. For example, a customer active in the stock market may wish frequent access to share and unit trust certificates. Also, if customers die, the bank can be asked to produce wills to the executors or solicitors so that these parties may act on the terms of the will. The will may contain details of funeral arrangements as well as instructions for the distribution of the estate.

Safe deposit facilities, where the customer holds a key to the safe deposit box or locker, would also be appropriate for frequent access but the customer can also maintain a degree of secrecy over the contents, although these facilities are only available in certain branches. It is also possible for an individual to rent a safe deposit box from a company which specialises in this type of service.

In practice, banks prefer sealed envelopes or locked boxes, with no indication of the contents. The exceptions to this include wills in sealed envelopes where the organisation would provide a receipt along the lines of: "Envelope closed with clear adhesive tape said to contain the will of …".

The safe custody service is used mainly by personal customers as many businesses, which have other assets or items of property to safeguard, tend to have their own safes or strong rooms for this purpose.

Many banks are no longer attracted to provide this service. As a result, the charges involved may be high and it could be that a bank will only provide these facilities to established safe custody customers.

Travel facilities

Foreign travel is very popular, with many individuals having two or more overseas holidays each year, and there has also been significant growth in business travel. It is also possible for customers to obtain both foreign currency and travellers' cheques from other providers – for example, the Post Office, travel agents, and a range of retail outlets. It is also possible to access these services online.

The main travel facilities offered are:

- purchase and sale of foreign currency
- traveller's cheques
- plastic cards
- travel insurance.

Purchase and sale of foreign currency

Foreign currency is cash and therefore is convenient to use but is not a safe form of money. It is useful when arriving in another country where it may not be convenient or possible to encash or use other forms of travel facilities immediately. A commission for the service of providing foreign currencies is made and a wide range is available. Whilst currency can be sold to customers before they make their trip, a bank will also buy back any unused foreign currency once the customer has returned home. Due to the high costs involved, only notes and not coins are bought and sold.

Travellers' cheques

Banks provide travellers' cheques in sterling and in most major currencies in a variety of denominations. The former are available immediately on payment of the appropriate commission. Most branches do not hold stocks of foreign currency traveller's cheques and they require to be obtained from head office or the International Department and either sent to the branch for collection or sent directly to the customer.

Travellers' cheques are widely accepted throughout the world in exchange for foreign currency or in payment for goods and services. The customer signs the travellers' cheques at the time of issue and then countersigns when they are used. Passport identification is usually required and an encashment fee is often charged.

Unlike foreign currency, lost or stolen cheques are refundable. Any unused travellers' cheques can be sold back to the bank by the customer after returning home.

Plastic cards

It is possible to use a range of plastic cards abroad – credit cards, charge cards and debit cards. These can be used to pay for goods and services and may also be used to obtain local currency from ATMs abroad. Prior to travelling, the customer should make the card issuer aware of where they will be travelling to and the duration of their stay – this is to avoid the risk of a transaction being declined as the card issuer suspects fraud.

Travel insurance

Financial setback, illness or stolen luggage are incidences of where customers are particularly vulnerable when travelling abroad but all the banks can arrange travel insurance through insurance companies.

Cover is provided in respect of:

- cancellation and curtailment charges (due to injury, illness of the insured, relative, etc)

- delayed departure (due to weather, transport failure, etc)

- loss of or damage to personal baggage (usually up to a maximum amount)

- loss of money, documents and passport (usually up to a maximum amount)

- personal accident (death, loss of limbs, etc)

- hospital benefit (in the event of the insured being hospitalised)

- medical expenses (particularly important in North America, for example, where the cost of medical assistance can be high)

- personal liability (indemnity against legal liability for accidental injury to third parties or for damage to their property)

- legal expenses and advice.

Although payment of travel costs by credit card provides some insurance cover, it is very limited.

Question   **2**

Go to question section starting on page 243

Check with the answer at the back of the book.

Review

Now consider the main learning points which were introduced in this chapter.

Go through them and tick each one when you are happy that you fully understand each point.

Then check back to the objectives at the beginning of the chapter and match them to the learning points.

Reread any section you are unsure of before moving on.

The difference between the saver and investor is their underlying attitude to risk. Savings are risk free and pay interest. Investments carry an element of risk, with the returns coming from dividend and/or capital growth.

☐

A current account is a traditional type of account which has been offered by banks for many years.

☐

There are a number of different current accounts now available on the market: ordinary, interest bearing, high interest, basic.

☐

ISAs are available to UK residents and can consist of cash or stocks and shares. There is no tax liability. There are annual limits on the amounts that can be paid in.

☐

Personal loans are normally granted for the purposes of consumer purchases.

☐

Banks are usually willing to lend customers a certain percentage of any equity in their homes provided that the bank is granted security over the house.

☐

Money transmission is the transfer of money from one party to another.

☐

A standing order is a signed authority given by a customer to a bank instructing the bank to make regular payments from the customer's account to a specified party at stated times for a stated period or until further notice.

☐

With a direct debit, the beneficiary instigates the debit and advises the bank of the amount involved.

☐

The Faster Payments service guarantees that automated payments will reach the beneficiary's account within two hours, although in reality receipt is almost instantaneous.

☐

A bank giro credit is a credit transfer form used by customers for making non-automated payments to accounts domiciled at a branch or bank other than the branch where the customer's account is held.

☐

A banker's draft is a cheque drawn on a bank.

☐

Customers may buy and sell shares through their bank.

☐

Banks can offer a service, usually through a specialist subsidiary company, to customers who wish their investments to be completely managed by the bank.

☐

An executor is someone who is appointed to ensure that the wishes of a deceased person, as set out in his or her will, are carried out.

☐

The difference between insurance and assurance is that assurance is concerned with certainty, insurance with possibility.

☐

Customers may lodge valuables and documents with many banks for safe keeping.

☐

The main travel facilities offered by banks are the purchase and sale of foreign currency and traveller's cheques, plastic cards and travel insurance.

☐

Key words in this chapter are given below. There is space to write your own revision notes and to add any other words or phrases that you want to remember.

current accounts

money transmission accounts

CHIP and PIN

Bank of England Monetary Policy Committee

interest bearing current account

deposit accounts

investment accounts

personal loans

credit scoring

house purchase loans

equity release/capital release loans

VOCA

Direct Debit Guarantee Scheme

banker's draft

safe custody

travel facilities

financial intermediation

second mortgage

lifetime mortgage

home reversion plan

Multiple choice questions   **2**

Try these self-test questions to assess your understanding of what you have read in this chapter.

The answers are at the back of the book.

1   Which one of the following is the best example of saving as opposed to investment?

    A   Benny, who is putting funds aside regularly to provide for his retirement

    B   Diane, who is building a fund to generate future income

    C   Meg, who is setting cash aside to buy a new car

    D   Hugh, who is building a portfolio of shares

2   Which one of the following is the best example of investment as opposed to saving?

    A   Betty, who is setting cash aside for her holidays

    B   Liz, who is building up a cash fund for "rainy day" purposes

    C   Beth, who is cutting expenditure because she is expecting a larger than usual mobile phone bill

    D   Lisa, who has opened a personal pension plan for her retirement

3   Which one of the following is most likely to be issued for use in conjunction with a current account?

    A   debit card

    B   VISA credit card

    C   charge card

    D   affinity card

Multiple choice questions   **2**

4 Overdrafts are normally repayable on which one of the following bases?

   A   subject to seven days' notice

   B   subject to one month's notice

   C   on demand

   D   by negotiation

5 VOCA facilitates the payment of which one of the following?

   A   both standing orders and direct debits

   B   standing orders but not direct debits

   C   direct debits but not standing orders

   D   neither standing orders nor direct debits

6 "A method of transferring funds by which the payee draws the funds electronically from the payer's bank." This is a description of which one of the following?

   A   bank giro credit

   B   banker's draft

   C   standing order

   D   direct debit

Multiple choice questions   **2**

7 Which one of the following would not be included on a completed bank giro credit form?

A   the reference number of the transferee

B   the party making the payment

C   the sorting code of the bank of the transferor

D   the amount to be paid

8 A contract note is used in connection with which one of the following types of banking service?

A   executor services

B   trustee services

C   share dealing services

D   investment advisory services

9 A person appointed to ensure that the wishes of a deceased person are carried out is known as:

A   a trustee

B   an administrator

C   an attorney

D   an executor

Multiple choice questions   **2**

10 An individual who holds and administers assets and property on behalf of another is known as:

A   a trustee

B   an administrator

C   an attorney

D   an executor

11 Which one of the following is an example of assurance as opposed to insurance?

A   a policy taken out by Maureen and Peter to cover their home and contents

B   a travel policy purchased by Nicola, who is going to Ibiza

C   a 25 year endowment policy taken out by Stephen on his own life

D   Sally's policy on her motor vehicle

12 Which one of the following statements is true?

A   assurance provides for events that may never happen

B   the most common types of assurance are for the home and the car

C   insurance provides a safeguard against things that may never happen

D   insurance and not assurance provides for events that will happen, such as death

Multiple choice questions   **2**

13   Retail banks usually offer investment and portfolio management services through which one of the following?

A   the internet

B   branch offices

C   specialist subsidiaries

D   agencies

3 Customers

Objectives

By the end of this chapter, you should be able to:

- Differentiate between the different classifications of customers.

- State the implications of dealing with different types of customers for the banker.

- Outline the basic anti-money laundering and data protection regulations.

Introduction

Having looked at the definition of a customer in the first chapter, now we'll take a closer look at the different types of customer who have dealings with a bank, recognising that different types of customers have different requirements and that different laws govern how they should operate in the community.

The banker therefore has to:

- recognise the category of customer he/she is dealing with

- know the requirements of a bank account for the particular type of customer.

The categories of customers we will look at here are:

- personal customers

- sole traders

- partnerships

- companies

- clubs, associations and societies

- trustees.

You should then have a basic understanding of the main features of these types of customers and how their bank accounts should operate, although we will take a closer look at operating customer accounts in the next chapter.

Personal customers

This type of customer is probably the most common type as the vast majority of bank accounts are held by individuals for personal use. Personal customers include individuals who hold savings accounts, current accounts, investment accounts, etc and also those who have mortgages with the bank or use insurance and other services the bank can provide.

Personal customers may have accounts in their own names or a joint account with one or more other individuals.

There are also bank accounts for business purposes and we will look at them later. For now we will concentrate on accounts opened for personal purposes.

There are not too many special considerations when dealing with bank accounts for individuals. Obviously individuals must comply with the laws of the land and a banker should always take care to ensure that bank accounts are not being used for illegal purposes. The main issues we will look at here are the differences between individual accounts and joint accounts and the special considerations that apply to a bank's dealings with individuals under the age of 18, but we will first look at the anti-money laundering regulations which must be complied with.

Anti-money laundering regulations

Money laundering is the process by which the proceeds of crime are converted into assets that seem to have a legitimate origin. The assets can either be retained permanently or recycled into further criminal activities. The objective is to take "dirty money" and by "washing" it through some legitimate means, such as using investments, removing it later as "clean money" – hence the term "money laundering".

In the past, banks have been unwitting accomplices in money laundering by unscrupulous persons who manage to disguise the origins of their funds by opening bogus business accounts or by passing money through legitimate businesses. The sums lodged to the business account are well in excess of what would normally be expected; for example, sums of say £500,000 being deposited every two or three weeks.

This may at first seem good business for the bank, but if the funds are being paid away to other parties or withdrawn by the customer, the bank will not obtain any benefit from the funds and could be facilitating money laundering. On the other hand, it may be perfectly normal for the business account to be conducted in this manner, but it is important for the bank to be aware of the type of business the customer is involved in so that the type of transactions that are likely to occur on the account can be anticipated.

In this case, if the bank had made initial enquiries and discovered that the customer acted as an agent for an overseas company engaged to purchase computer software, it may be perfectly normal for large sums to be deposited in the account from time to time. However, if you knew that the customer had a small newsagent's shop, you would expect to see a very different pattern of lodgements to and withdrawals from the account.

The UK regulations require that financial institutions:

- ask all new customers to prove their identity

- check the sources of any one-off transactions exceeding £10,000 (€15,000)

- check the sources of separate or linked transactions over £10,000

- keep adequate records showing evidence of the client's identity and transactions for five years; this provision still applies even if the customer has subsequently closed the account

- maintain internal reporting procedures with one member of staff responsible for receiving reports of suspicious transactions who should inform and cooperate with the police.

Firms should have suitable training programmes in place to make staff aware not only of the policies and procedures, but also of the legal requirements.

There is also an offence of "failing to disclose knowledge or suspicion of money laundering" if:

- a person knows of, or suspects someone to be engaged in money laundering even if that knowledge or suspicion is based on it coming to his attention in the course of his trade, profession, etc

- he does not report it to the Police or HM Revenue and Customs as soon as is reasonably practicable.

Disclosure does not constitute a breach of customer confidentiality as discussed in Chapter 1.

While there should be a specific individual in the organisation – the Money Laundering Reporting Officer (MLRO) – who is responsible for monitoring potentially suspicious transactions, all staff have a legal obligation to report any suspicious applications or transactions to the MLRO. In such instances, a Suspicious Transaction Report (STR) should be completed and then reported to the Serious Organised Crime Agency

(SOCA). Once an STR has been lodged, the lender has an obligation not to "tip off" the individual who is the subject of the STR.

The penalties relating to money laundering are:

- Any individual providing assistance to obtain, conceal or invest the proceeds of crime – maximum 14 years' imprisonment, a fine, or both

- Any individual failing to report a suspicious transaction, or tipping off the customer – maximum 5 years' imprisonment, a fine, or both

- Any individual failing to comply with the Money Laundering Regulations – maximum 2 years' imprisonment, a fine, or both

The organisation must have processes and procedures in place that identify all deposits that are greater than a predefined amount; these transactions should be investigated to determine the source of the funds.

An individual's identity is defined as:

- name

- address at which the person can be found, including the postcode

- date of birth.

Verification must take place within a reasonable time and two separate forms of verification should be used. You will be familiar with this as your bank will have procedures in place for verifying a customer's identity when they wish to open a new account, etc. The customer's name and address should be verified independently from a range of documents that are acceptable for this purpose. Many banks now use automated identity and address verification systems.

The types of documents we look for include:

- driving licence

- credit/debit cards

- passport

- recent utility bill.

In addition to this verification, a credit reference check should also be carried out. If an application is received by post, phone, fax or the internet, these requirements must still be met.

"Due diligence" is the term given to describe these identity checks and the "Know your Customer" information gleaned by a bank, which describes the appropriate additional information the bank needs in order to understand the customer's circumstances.

Data Protection Acts 1984 and 1998

The *Data Protection Act 1984* was primarily intended to create rights for data subjects to protect their privacy. The Act only covered personal data which is automatically processed and did not cover the processing of personal data by manual methods nor did it include information relating to corporate bodies. The *1998 Act* replaced the *1984 Act* to implement the European Data Protection Directive. It serves to widen the responsibilities of data controllers and gives new rights to data subjects. The new Act came into force at the end of 1999.

The *1998 Act* extends data protection to manual records, covering personal data recorded or intended to be recorded as part of a "relevant filing system" so certain types of manual files will be affected.

■ Definitions

The definitions used in the Act are:

- "data" is any information recorded in a form that can be processed either manually or automatically by computer, and information that is manually recorded with the intention of processing it on a computer at some future point

- "personal data" is any data that relates to a living individual who can be identified; this definition has been widened to include sole traders, partners, directors and shareholders

- "sensitive data" is data covering race, religion, political issues, health and gender, and criminal or allegedly criminal offences

- a "data controller" is any person (or company) who holds data and determines the purpose and nature of processing

- a "data subject" is the person to whom the data relates

- "processing data" means obtaining, amending, augmenting, deleting, rearranging or extracting data; this must be done in accordance with the eight data protection principles (listed below).

■ Registration

All data controllers and computer bureaux must register with the Information Commissioner who is the government official responsible for enforcing the Act.

The information that must be registered is:

- a description of the personal data being or to be processed by or on behalf of the data controller and of the category of data subject to which they relate

- a description of the purpose or purposes for which the data are being or are to be processed

- a description of those persons to whom it is intended to disclose or may wish to disclose personal data

- details of any countries outside the European Economic Area to which it is intended to transfer personal data either directly or indirectly.

■ Data protection principles

There are eight principles for handling personal data:

1 Personal data shall be processed fairly and lawfully which means that the person supplying the information should not be misled nor deceived as to why it is being sought or as to the use(s) to which it may be put. In the case of sensitive data, the data subject must give his explicit consent to the processing of the personal data otherwise it can only be processed in certain very limited circumstances.

2 Personal data shall be obtained only for one or more specified and lawful purpose(s) and shall not be further processed in any manner incompatible with that purpose.

3 Personal data shall be adequate, relevant and not excessive in relation to the purpose or purposes for which they are processed

which means that there must be a reason for obtaining each piece of information from a data subject.

4   Personal data shall be accurate and, where necessary, kept up to date.

5   Personal data processed for any purpose or purposes should not be kept any longer than is necessary for that purpose or those purposes.

6   Personal data shall be processed in accordance with the rights of data subjects under the Act.

7   Appropriate security measures should be taken against unauthorised access to or alteration, disclosure or destruction of personal data and against accidental loss or destruction of personal data.

8   Personal data shall not be transferred to any country outside the European Economic Area which does not provide adequate protection for personal data.

■ **Rights of data subjects**

The rights of data subjects are:

- access to the personal data when requested in writing

- prevent processing likely to cause damage or distress

- prevent processing for the purposes of direct marketing

- claim compensation for damage caused through non-compliance by the data controller

- rectify, block, insist on erasure or destruction of inaccurate data

- have automatic decisions taken on the basis of their data which significantly affect them.

Joint accounts

When an account is opened in the names of two or more customers, strictly speaking operations on the account can only be on the authority of all the parties to the account which would obviously be totally impractical for a great number of a bank's customers.

Example

If a husband and wife maintain a joint account, it would be difficult for one of them to go shopping on their own as they would both have to be present to sign a cheque. Similarly, it would not be possible for the bank to offer them a facility whereby they could make use of the bank's automatic cash dispensing machines as this involves issuing a card which can only be used by one person at a time. To make life simpler, our couple could authorise the bank to accept the instructions of either one of them by signing a mandate authorising the bank to pay cheques, accept standing order instructions, requests to transfer funds to an another account and permit withdrawals if the cheque or instruction is signed by only one of them.

The mandate should be signed by all the parties to the account. It is important that the customers appreciate what the mandate entails as it would be possible for one party to pay a large amount of cash into the bank account only to have it withdrawn by the other party without his/her knowledge. In such circumstances, the bank would not wish to become involved in any arguments between the customers and can point to the mandate held.

This type of situation could be even more troublesome if the account became overdrawn as a result of one of the parties taking money out of the account. This entails the concept of joint and several liability. If authority has been obtained in terms of a mandate to allow operations on an account by one or more of the account holders, they are still only liable jointly if the account becomes overdrawn; that is, each party is only liable for their share of the debt.

Joint and several liability means that, while the parties to the account may between themselves consider they are only liable for their share of any debt, as far as the bank is concerned, each party will be held liable for the full amount of the debt. In most cases, the joint account mandate will contain an undertaking that the parties will be jointly and severally liable, although this authority could be contained within a separate document. A bank should also hold an authority from parties to a joint account stating that each party to the account will be jointly and severally liable even where no authority is held for joint and several operations on the account.

> ## Example
>
> The bank could be in a position where a joint account has been allowed to become overdrawn to the extent of £10,000 on the strength of the wealth of one of the parties to the account. If the parties are only jointly liable, the bank could only look to each party for £5,000, meaning that it would be difficult to recover the £5,000 due by the party with little means. From the bank's point of view, it would be better if they could pursue the wealthy party for the full £10,000 and this could be done if both parties were jointly and severally liable for any indebtedness on the account.

Customers under the age of 18

The law recognises that people of a certain age may not be fully aware of the consequences of entering into certain transactions and that such persons should be protected by law in case they are taken advantage of. Whilst young people have no legal capacity, they are permitted to enter into a transaction that is deemed a normal transaction for people of that age to enter into. As a result, it is possible for young people to hold bank accounts in their own name – as this is felt to be a normal transaction for such a person. Indeed, many banks have designed special accounts tailored to the needs of young people.

However, it is not proper for banks to send a young person under the age of 18 information regarding credit facilities, and for this reason, it would not be normal for a bank to grant credit to anyone under this age.

Business customers

As well as personal customers, banks have a great number of business customers. Customers can conduct business on their own as sole traders or be in business with one or more other persons in partnership, or they can form a limited company. It is extremely important to recognise which type of business is being dealt with as each is subject to different laws and requirements.

Sole traders

In most respects there is no difference in the manner in which a bank should conduct its dealings with an individual opening an account for business purposes or for personal purposes. It is important, however, to ensure that the accounts of the customer and any cheque books issued detail the customer accurately.

Example

If your customer owns a small newsagents shop called "News International" it would not be appropriate for the bank account to be styled "News International" as this particular entity does not exist, it is only a trading name. Similarly it could be misleading to the public, especially other businesses supplying goods to your customer on credit if they thought they were dealing with a major business called "News International". If your customer's name is James Robertson, he should let everyone know that they are dealing with James Robertson **trading as** "News International" which is also how the bank accounts and cheque books should be styled.

It is also important to bear this in mind when having your customer execute any deeds, especially documents in terms of which security is being granted to the bank over any assets. As "News International" does not actually exist, therefore it will not own any assets. The shop and all of the stock actually belong to James Robertson, just as any debts to bankers and suppliers are due by James Robertson.

Some customers will have their accounts styled "Business Account", such as "James Robertson – Business Account" which is perfectly acceptable for cheque books so that the public can see that they are dealing with an individual.

The advantages of being a sole trader include that:

- it is the simplest business model to set up – all that needs to be done is open the business account and advise HM Revenue and Customs within three months of starting to trade

- the owner has full control over the business – there is no one else involved with the business to consult when making decisions

- there is no need to go to the expense of using an accountant – although many sole traders will make a commercial decision to do so.

The disadvantages of setting up as a sole trader are that:

- the owner is personally liable for all of the debts of the business, therefore if things go wrong and the business fails with debts, the owner must repay the businesses creditors

- to be successful, the sole trader must be multi-skilled, not only in the activity of the business but also in managing the business

- taking time off or being ill may have a detrimental effect on the business, although the sole trader may employ other people to work in the business; being a sole trader means that there is only one owner of the business. Whilst there is only one owner of the business, this does not preclude the owner from employing staff.

Partnerships

If two or more people are trading together in an attempt to make profits, then in terms of the *Partnership Act 1890* they are in partnership.

Example

James and his wife own the newsagent shop and work in it together. They may not have set out to form a partnership or realise that they are a partnership or a firm, but the simple fact that they are trading together for profit makes them a partnership. Their bank accounts should therefore show the firm's name.

If your customers did not realise that they were in partnership, they will probably not have thought of a firm name. The most likely firm names in this case would be "Firm of James and Elizabeth Robertson" or "Firm of News International" or "Firm of the Robertsons" or "Firm of James and Elizabeth Robertson trading as News International".

Again it is important that members of the public and other businesses know who they are dealing with. Partnerships as well as individuals are subject to the *Business Names Act 1985*. In the case of partnerships, they must state legibly on all business letters, orders to suppliers and similar documents issued in the course of business, the name of each partner of the firm.

If your branch or department regularly receives letters from solicitors or accountants, two very common types of firms, take a look at their letter paper and you will see that the names of the partners are shown somewhere on the letter.

All the partners' names do not need to be shown on cheques issued by a firm.

Partnership agreements and partnership mandates

It is usual for partners in a firm to draw up a partnership agreement or a contract of co-partnery setting out the relationship and the arrangements that have been agreed between the parties. This partnership agreement will cover such matters as how the profits (and any losses) of the firm will be apportioned and how the assets of the firm will be divided in the event of the firm being dissolved.

It is not essential for the partners to draw up a partnership agreement and it is not necessary for the banker to see a partnership agreement before a bank account can be opened in name of the firm. The relationship between the bank and the firm will be set out in the partnership mandate or partnership letter. This authority should be addressed to the bank and be signed by all of the partners in the firm. In addition to having each partner sign the letter, the bank should also obtain specimens of how each partner will sign cheques and other orders on behalf of the firm; for example, James Robertson may wish to sign cheques "Firm of News International".

The mandate will also set out how many partners are required to sign cheques issued by the firm. Usually cheques are signed by any one partner, but occasionally it is requested that cheques be signed by all of the partners or any two partners or a particular partner and any other partner or two partners, one of whom must be any one of X, Y or Z with the other being any one of A, B, C, D or E.

There are other alternatives, the most important consideration for the banker being that the instructions are clear so that there is no risk of a cheque being paid that has not been signed properly. The partnership letter should also authorise the bank to permit overdrafts on the account if this is anticipated.

Liability of partners

Every partner in a firm is liable jointly and severally for all debts and obligations of the firm incurred while he/she is a partner. The estate of a deceased partner is liable for the debts of a firm due at the date of death which means that creditors can look beyond the assets of the firm if they still remain unpaid after all such assets have been realised; they could, for example, take legal action to take possession of the dwelling house of one of the partners.

A firm is a legal person, distinct from the partners. The firm has its own assets and each time there is a change in the make up of the partners, either by the death or resignation of an existing partner or by the admission of a new partner, a new firm is effectively created. It is therefore necessary to renew mandates and other authorities held from the firm.

A new partner is not liable for debts of the old firm and cannot be held liable for anything done before he/she becomes a partner. A retiring partner remains liable for debts incurred while he/she was a partner but will not be liable for any debts incurred by the firm after he/she has notified the relevant party that he/she has ceased to be a partner. A partner who retires should therefore give notice to the bank in order to avoid being held jointly and severally liable for debts incurred after his/her retirement.

Where the bank wishes to make an incoming partner liable for the existing debts of the firm, the firm's account should be closed by paying into the account the amount of the overdraft. The cheque issued to clear the overdraft should preferably be signed by all of the partners of the firm, including the new partner, and should be debited to a new account in name of the firm.

As each partner in a firm is jointly and severally liable for the debts of the firm, the bank may lend to a firm solely on the strength of the assets of one of the partners. If this partner were to resign from the firm, it is obviously important that he/she remains liable for the debts of the firm incurred while he/she was a partner. This partner will not be liable for any new debts incurred by the firm after his/her resignation.

To protect its position against the outgoing partner or the estate of a deceased partner, it is essential that the bank stops operations on the firm's bank account. This situation arose in what became known as Clayton's case and the ruling made there often applies to similar situations occurring today.

Clayton's Case

As far as a current account is concerned, the rule in Clayton's case states that the first in/first out principle should apply, in accordance with the dates of the transactions in the account.

In the current or running account, the sum first paid in is deemed to be the first drawn out, and, the earliest item on the debit side is extinguished or reduced by the first item on the credit side.

Example 1 – John Cavanagh Current Account		Dr	Cr	Balance
		£	£	£
April 1				Dr 500
April 3	Cash		200 (A)	Dr 300
April 4	Cash		300 (B)	Nil
April 8	Cheque	400		Dr 400
April 10	Cheque	500		Dr 900
April 12	Cash		400 (C)	Dr 500
April 16	Cheque	600		Dr 1,100

The rule in Clayton's case will operate as follows:

1. Item A partly extinguishes the opening £500 debit balance (£500 to £300 Dr).

2. Item B totally extinguishes the opening £500 debit balance (£300 to Nil).

3. Item C extinguishes the debit entry of April 8th (i.e. £400).

4. The debit balance on the 12th is made up by the debit item on the 10th.

Case study

CLAYTON'S CASE
Devaynes -v- Noble, 1816

Devaynes, one of the partners in a banking business, died, but the firm of Devaynes, Dawes, Noble, Croft and Barwick continued business under the same name. At the time of Devaynes's death the firm owed Nathaniel Clayton £1,713 – the credit balance on Clayton's account. Shortly afterwards the firm went bankrupt. Between the time of Devaynes's death and the firm's bankruptcy, Clayton continued to operate on his account, withdrawing and paying in funds. His total withdrawals (although offset by deposits) during this time amounted to more than £1,713. Clayton, on the bankruptcy of the firm, claimed against Devaynes's estate for the amount due to him at the date of Devaynes's death i.e. £1,713. But transactions had since taken place on the account. It was shown that the total drawings since Devaynes's death exceeded the balance of £1,713 and that the credit balance at the date of the firm's bankruptcy comprised fresh monies subsequently paid in.

Clayton's claim was not accepted. The estate of Devaynes, the deceased partner, should not be liable.

Example 2 – Betty Brown and Greg McPherson
Joint Account
(Joint and Several liability agreed)

		Dr £	Cr £	Balance £
May 1	Balance			Dr 500
May 3	Cash		200 (A)	Dr 300
May 4	Cash		300 (B)	Nil
May 8	Cheque	400		Dr 400
May 10	Cheque	500		Dr 900
May 12	Cash		400 (C)	Dr 500
May 16	Cheque	600		Dr 1,100

In this example, if the bank receives notification of Brown's death on 11 May and stops operations on the account, then given the joint and several liability of the parties, the bank has recourse to the deceased's estate for the outstanding debit balance at that point, £900.

What if the Bank does not stop the Account but allows it to continue?

- The credit entry on the 12 May (£400) extinguishes part of the liability on Brown's estate (£900 down to £500).

- So although the debit balance on 16 May is £1,100, Brown's estate is only liable for £500.

- The debit on the 16 May constitutes new borrowing (£600) for which Brown's estate is not liable.

If further transactions took place before operations on the account were stopped, eventually the debit balance which existed at the date the bank received notice of death (£900) would be fully cleared by future credits.

If this happened the bank could claim nothing from the deceased's estate and would have to rely solely upon the survivor for repayment of any debt.

You can see the problems this might cause to the bank if the survivor, Greg McPherson, was unable to repay.

If the bank wishes to preserve rights against the deceased's estate for liability at the date of death, the account should be stopped on notice of death, otherwise that liability will be reduced or extinguished.

Limited liability partnerships

A limited liability partnership (LLP) is a legal entity which is separate from its members in that each member of an LLP acts as an agent for the partnership. LLPs are not governed by the law relating to partnerships, but have their own relevant law in the *Limited Liability Partnerships Act 2000* and in the *Limited Liability Partnerships Regulations 2001*.

LLPs should not be confused with limited partnerships. An LLP must be registered at Companies House in the same way as for an incorporated company and will continue in existence as long as it remains registered and has at least two members. Unlike incorporated companies, an LLP does not have a Memorandum or Articles of Association.

An LLP and any negligent members are liable to the full extent of their assets while the liability of the other members will be limited. The rights and duties of members to one another and to the LLP are governed by a confidential agreement between the members which does not have to be in writing. Profits are shared amongst the members of the LLP, and the individual members (and not the LLP) pay income tax on these profits. Unlike limited companies, LLPs do not pay corporation tax.

In most cases the members will be self employed, so they must include details of any profits they receive or share on their individual self assessment tax returns each year. Self employed partners are also responsible for paying their own National Insurance Contributions. It is important that each member of the LLP should register as self employed with HM Revenue and Customs.

The advantages of a partnership are that:

- like a sole trader, it is fairly straightforward to set up, although HM Revenue and Customs must be advised within three months of the partnership starting to trade

- as with the sole trader, there is no need to use the services of an accountant, although many partnerships will choose to use such a service

- there is shared responsibility and so different partners may specialise in running different parts of the business depending on their individual skills and expertise, such as one partner dealing with administration, another marketing, and a third focusing on the production of the product or service the partnership trades in.

The disadvantages of a partnership include:

- the joint and several liability discussed earlier – although note that this relates to general partnerships and not the LLPs that have just been discussed.

- the stresses and strains of having to involve other partners in the decision making process, such as when disagreements arise.

Limited companies

The main features of a limited company are that it is a separate and distinct legal entity from its members and that the liability of the members is limited. A company's members are its shareholders and there can be as few as one member. Each member invests money in the company by purchasing shares in the company. The only liability that a member of a company has for the debts of the company is to pay any unpaid amounts due on the shares he or she has purchased. This means that anyone dealing with the company, including banks and suppliers, must look only to the assets of the company and can have no claim on the assets of the members.

You can see how this type of arrangement will be attractive to individuals but less attractive to those dealing with the company which is why, when lending to limited companies, a bank will sometimes look for a personal guarantee from the directors, usually supported by a charge over some other asset, such as their dwelling houses.

Public companies and private companies

Companies can be either public or private. Public companies are generally larger and their shares may be bought and sold on the stock exchange. The requirements for forming a public company are much stricter than those for forming a private company. The name of a public company ends with "Public Limited Company", "PLC" or "plc", whereas the name of a private company ends with "Limited" or "Ltd".

In this course we will be looking only at private companies.

Incorporation

The issue by the Registrar of Companies of a Certificate of Incorporation is conclusive evidence of a company's existence and that all the requirements of the *Companies Acts* on incorporation have been complied with.

The Certificate of Incorporation shows:

- the name of the company (ending with the word "Limited")

- the company number (unique to the company)

- whether the Certificate has been issued by the Registrar in Edinburgh (Scottish company) or Cardiff (English/Welsh company).

As the company is a separate legal entity from its shareholders, the Certificate of Incorporation is the equivalent of a birth certificate. If, after incorporation, a company changes its name, the Registrar will issue a Certificate of Incorporation on Change of Name. The Registrar may refuse to accept the name if, for example, there is already in existence a company with the same name or something very similar.

The directors

The business and affairs of a company are managed by the directors of the company who are elected by the members of the company. A private company may have at least one director and a Secretary, although it is possible for one person to be both director and Secretary . In practice it is sometimes the case that the company's Secretary will be the customer's solicitor or accountant.

Memorandum of Association

The Memorandum of Association is a statement made by each of the subscribers (these are the original shareholders in the company), stating that they intend to form a company and become a member of that company. Assuming that the company will issue shares, the subscribers agree to take at least one share.

Articles of Association

The Articles are the rules that govern the internal dealings of the company that the shareholders and officers (the Directors and Company Secretary) agree to. It is possible for a company to adopt the standard Articles provided by Companies House, or they can draft their own. Should the company choose that latter option, then the Articles that they use can be adapted from the model Articles. However, should the model Articles not be used in their entirety, then any customised Articles must not include any provision that breaks the law.

The advantages of a limited company are that:

- the liability of its members is limited

- it may be a more tax-efficient way for some individuals to set up their business

- in some areas of work, being a limited company may give the business added credibility, such as in activities where subcontracting is the norm.

The disadvantages of a limited company include:

- the setting up costs are higher compared to a sole trader or partnership

- some information about the company is available to the public via Companies House

- it is necessary to use the services of an accountant at certain times of the year.

Clubs, associations and societies

It is also possible to come across the situation where the bank is dealing with a voluntary association that seeks to promote a common interest other than making profit – for example, a golf club or a pressure group. Such unincorporated bodies have no legal personality and can only raise a legal action, or be sued in the names of the members.

The main problem for banks in dealing with such accounts is to ensure that it holds proper authority for operations on the account in terms of the constitution of the association, and that where overdraft facilities are granted; responsibility for the amount involved is fixed, either on the association or on individual members.

When someone becomes a member of a club, they accept the rules of the club. The liability of a member of a club or association for its debts will depend on the terms of the constitution, although in practice unless the member has specifically agreed to accept liability, or has acted as an agent of the association, it may be difficult to establish that they are liable for the debts of the association.

The members of clubs and associations usually act through their appointed office bearers and their committees. When dealing with an unincorporated body, and especially when lending to it, the bank should ask for a copy of the rules and constitution of the association. The constitution must be carefully examined to ascertain to what extent the members of the club or association or society have granted powers to act as office bearers and committees.

An excerpt minute, consistent with the terms of the association's constitution and rules, should be obtained of the meeting of the members, or of the appropriate committee of the club, resolving that the bank account is to be kept at the bank and containing full instructions regarding the powers of the persons who have been appointed to operate the account. There may be small clubs with no sets of rules, but if the bank has obtained a document, in the form of an excerpt minute and signed by the office bearers, the bank should be able to accept the document as a proper authority.

The opening of accounts in the name of individuals on behalf of associations should not be encouraged. Difficulties could arise if the individual dies, as any sum standing to the credit of the account forms part of the deceased's estate and can only be uplifted by their executors.

Given the potential difficulties in establishing who is liable for the debts of an association or club, overdraft facilities should only be granted against tangible security such as a charge over the association's premises or clubhouse or against the joint and several guarantee of some of the members or the committee who are considered by the bank to be good for the sum involved.

Trustees

A trustee is someone who has been appointed to hold and administer property for the use of third parties. For example, if someone dies leaving a young family, or if someone wishes to make provision for their family when they are not yet capable of looking after their own financial affairs, they may create a trust for their benefit and pay money into the trust or transfer assets, such as a property, into the ownership of the trust.

The document creating the trust is called a trust deed and in terms of the trust deed someone will be appointed to administer the affairs of the trust for the benefit of the beneficiaries of the trust.

Another example of a trust is a company pension scheme. A company will transfer funds to the pension scheme and the funds will be looked after and invested by the trustee(s) to provide pensions for the employees of the company when they retire.

If a bank is requested to open an account in the name of a trustee, it should first see a copy of the trust deed setting out the powers and responsibilities of the trustee(s). Trustees may only borrow from the bank if they have the power to do so. The powers of a trustee will be set out in the trust deed itself, although in terms of Section 4 of the *Trusts (Scotland) Act 1921*, trustees are empowered to borrow on the security of the assets of the trust for purposes which are in the interests of the trust.

Question   **3**

Go to question section starting on page 243

Check with the answer at the back of the book.

Review

Now consider the main learning points which were introduced in this chapter.

Go through them and tick each one when you are happy that you fully understand each point.

Then check back to the objectives at the beginning of the chapter and match them to the learning points.

Reread any section you are unsure of before moving on.

Money laundering is the process by which the proceeds of crime are converted into assets that seem to have a legitimate origin.

☐

Banks must comply with certain anti-money laundering regulations when opening and running customers' accounts.

☐

Joint and several liability means that each party to an account will be held liable for the full amount of the debt.

☐

If an individual is carrying on business in his own name and has not formed a limited company, this person is deemed to be a sole trader.

☐

If two or more people are trading together in an attempt to make profits and have not formed a limited company, they are deemed to be a partnership.

☐

Clayton's case states that, when dealing with a running account which is in debt, any lodgement made will extinguish, or party extinguish, the oldest debt.

☐

A limited company is a separate and distinct legal entity from its members and that the liability of the members is limited.

☐

A Certificate of Incorporation is conclusive evidence of a company's existence and that all the requirements of the Companies Acts on incorporation have been complied with.

 Key words in this chapter are given below. There is space to write your own revision notes and to add any other words or phrases that you want to remember.

money laundering

suspicious transaction report

joint and several liability

sole trader

partnership

limited company

Clayton's Case

limited liability partnerships

Certificate of Incorporation

unincorporated bodies

Articles of Association

Multiple choice questions   **3**

Try these self-test questions to assess your understanding of what you have read in this chapter.

The answers are at the back of the book.

1   A person under the age of 18 may enter into a transaction subject to which one of the following?

    A   Agreement of a parent or guardian

    B   The transaction being a common one for a young person to enter into

    C   The transaction being regulated by the Consumer Credit Acts

    D   Under no circumstances

2   Judith and Ray have a loan in joint names. They owe £5,000 in total. If Judith dies, Ray is liable for the whole debt, and vice versa. Legally their obligation is:

    A   joint

    B   several

    C   joint or several

    D   joint and several

3   For a bank, the main difference between dealing with an individual and dealing with a sole trader is which one of the following?

    A   the sole trader's interest is treated differently for income tax purposes

    B   the sole trader carries limited liability whilst the individual does not

    C   the sole trader's assets are protected by specific legislation

    D   there is no difference in the manner in which the bank conducts its dealings with either

Multiple choice questions   3

4 Which one of the following statements is true in the context of partnership accounts?

    A   all partners are normally severally liable

    B   it is not necessary for all the names of the partners to be shown on cheques

    C   there is no need for a mandate to define the signatories

    D   a partnership letter need only be signed by the senior partners

5 Jock is about to retire as a partner in his firm. Which one of the following statements is true?

    A   Jock will remain liable for debts incurred by the firm while he was a partner but will not be liable for debts incurred after notification of retirement

    B   Jock will incur no liability for any debts once he retires

    C   Jock will be liable for all debts incurred by the partnership before and after his retirement

    D   Jock may rescind his liability for all debts as long as he does so in writing to all the partners

6 Which one of the following is the correct term to be used in the name of a private limited company?

    A   plc

    B   and Co

    C   limited

    D   incorporated

Multiple choice questions   **3**

7 Which one of the following issues a Certificate of Incorporation?

   A   Department of Trade and Industry

   B   Secretary of the company to be incorporated

   C   Directors of the company to be incorporated

   D   Registrar of Companies

8 The Memorandum of Association is a statement made by which one of the following?

   A   The Directors

   B   The current shareholders

   C   The original shareholders

   D   The Registrar of Companies

9 The rules for the internal management of a limited company may be found in which one of the following?

   A   Memorandum of Association and the Certificate of Incorporation

   B   Articles of Association and the Memorandum of Association

   C   Memorandum of Association only

   D   Articles of Association only

Multiple choice questions   **3**

10 The shareholders of a limited company are referred to in company law as:

A   promoters

B   members

C   directors

D   creditors

11 If a limited company is wound up, the liability of the shareholders is:

A   Nil

B   Unlimited

C   Determined in proportion to their shareholding

D   Restricted to any unpaid amount on party-paid shares

12 Which one of the following best describes the officers of a company?

A   The Directors and the Company Secretary

B   The senior management team

C   All current shareholders

D   The Chief Executive Officer and the Company Secretary

Multiple choice questions   **3**

13 The maximum number of people who may form a voluntary association to promote a common interest is which one of the following?

A   ten

B   twenty

C   fifty

D   there is no maximum

14 The manner in which profits are to be divided between partners is set out in which one of the following?

A   Memorandum of Association

B   Articles of Association

C   partnership agreement

D   partnership letter

15 You receive a cheque drawn on "The Firm of News International". This indicates that the bank account is conducted on behalf of which one of the following?

A   a private limited company

B   a partnership

C   a sole trader

D   an association

4 Operating Customer Accounts

Objectives

By the end of this chapter, you should be able to:

- Explain why banks need to ingather information on both new and existing customers.

- State why accounts may be closed and describe what should be done to close an unsatisfactory account.

- Outline the actions to be taken on receipt of notice of the death of a customer.

- Describe the actions to be taken to control accounts, including the work of collections and recoveries departments.

- Explain why banks charge certain customers.

Introduction

We have just looked at the types of customers that will come into contact with a bank and at some special considerations and requirements that the banker should bear in mind when dealing with such customers. Now we'll take a more general look at the operation of customers' accounts, at the bank's requirements when a bank account is opened or closed and at what action should be taken by a bank on being notified of the death of a customer.

We'll then go on to look at why and how a bank monitors operations on a customer's account, particularly accounts on which borrowing facilities have been granted and consider one or two of the possible options when a customer is unable or unwilling to repay borrowing facilities. We'll end with a brief look at the charges levied by banks for their services.

Opening accounts

When a bank account is opened it is vitally important for the bank to obtain as much information as possible about the new customer, particularly if borrowing facilities are being contemplated. You will also recall from the last chapter that banks must obtain specific information from a prospective customer to comply with anti-money laundering regulations. The name given to the checks carried out by a bank when opening an account or obtaining information to support a lending application is called "due diligence".

A bank is not obliged to accept anyone as a customer and it would be unwise to open an account unless the bank is completely satisfied as to the character and standing of the applicant. As much information as possible about a new customer can be obtained by using standardised application to open account forms as well as carrying out some form of customer profiling at the same time.

Customer profiling is an activity where the bank finds out as much information as possible about a customer's circumstances, their background and aspirations. This information is usually stored electronically and is updated during each meeting with the customer. The information contained within the profile is used to match the bank's products and services to the needs and wants of the individual customer.

It has been held that a banker who fails to take proper precautions when an account is opened has acted with negligence. Where a banker, in good faith and without negligence, credits a customer's account with a cheque and then receives payment of the cheque from the bank on which the cheque was drawn, and it later transpires that the customer who lodged the cheque did not have proper title to it, the banker does not incur any liability to the true owner of the cheque.

In addition to obtaining all the necessary information about a new customer before any operations can be permitted on the account, the bank must also arrange an appropriate mandate which will govern how operations on the account are conducted.

Case studies

Ladbroke -v- Todd, 1914

A cheque was stolen from a pillar box by a third party who impersonated the payee and opened a bank account with the cheque. The bank made no enquiries as to the new customer's identity or character and was therefore held to have acted negligently and was liable to reimburse the true owner of the cheque.

Savory & Company -v- Lloyds Bank, 1932

Two stockbroker's clerks who had stolen cheques belonging to their employers paid the cheques into bank accounts. In one case a cheque was paid into an account in the name of the clerk and in the other the cheque was paid into an account in the name of the wife of the clerk. The court held that there was negligence on the part of the bank in both cases because it did not obtain proper references. In the case where the cheque was lodged to an account in the name of the wife of one of the thieves, the bank was held to be negligent as, at the time the account was opened, it did not obtain the name of the customer's husband and details of his employment.

In the case of an account in the name of two or more customers, it is usual for a mandate to be granted in favour of the bank permitting operations on the account by any one of the parties. You will recall that the bank should also be granted an undertaking by the customers that each one of them will be jointly and severally liable for repayment of any indebtedness that may occur. If two or more customers are jointly and severally liable for a debt, it means that each person is liable for the full amount of the debt.

If the bank does not have an undertaking from the customers that they will be jointly and severally liable for repayment of the debt, in the case of an account in the name of three customers, each customer would be liable for a third of the debt which could be detrimental to the interests of the bank, especially if only one of the customers had the means to repay the debt.

In the case of a partnership wishing to open an account, the bank must obtain a partnership account letter or mandate. Each partner in a firm is jointly and severally liable for the indebtedness of the firm but the position will be put beyond doubt by taking a partnership mandate.

When an account is to be opened in the name of a limited company, the bank should obtain an excerpt minute from the meeting of the directors of the company at which it was resolved that a bank account be opened and how operations on the account should be conducted. The bank will usually supply the company with a standard opening account form which is, in effect, an excerpt minute from the directors' meeting.

The bank should also obtain sight of the company's Certificate of Incorporation which is conclusive evidence that all of the requirements for incorporation of a company have been complied with and that the company is in fact in existence.

Operations on customers' accounts

Provided that all the necessary stages have been completed for opening an account, a customer's account should operate smoothly and not be a cause for concern. Operations on customers' accounts should nevertheless be monitored, as often this is the best way of keeping informed of changes in the customer's circumstances and may provide an early warning that a customer is in financial difficulty.

If overdraft facilities have been permitted on the account or if any other borrowing facilities have been permitted, it is vital to monitor operations on the customer's account at all times to be satisfied as to the safety of the advance that has been granted. If there are early warning signs that things are not as they should be, action can be taken to assist the customer and at the same time protect the bank from loss. We shall look at the control and monitoring of accounts later.

You will remember that a partner is only liable for the debts of a firm incurred while he was a partner and later you will discover that if a bank has a charge (or security) over a property and is subsequently advised that some other party has been granted a charge over the same property, the bank's charge will only cover sums outstanding at the time the creation of the second charge is intimated.

In both sets of circumstances, unless in the case of a second charge being granted, the only borrowing secured by the charge stands for reduction only – such as a house purchase loan or a term loan – it will be necessary for the bank to stop operations on the account in order to preserve its position.

If operations are allowed to continue, any lodgements to the account will reduce the amount secured by the charge or due by the retiring partner and any further withdrawals will be classed as *nova debita* (new debt) and will not be covered by the charge or be capable of being due by the retiring partner.

It is important therefore that if during the course of operations on any account anything happens which involves a change in the parties liable for a debt or the obligations secured by any item of security, it is essential that operations are stopped to preserve the bank's position and to prevent the rule in Clayton's case from working to the detriment of the bank.

Closing accounts

There are several reasons why an account may be closed, such as:

- the account may have become dormant and it is convenient for the bank for the account to be closed

- the customer may wish to close the account and will have a variety of reasons for doing so.

In such circumstances it is quite straightforward and all that will be required is for the customer to withdraw the balance of the account. In the case of a current account, the customer should be requested to return the cheque book. Any plastic cards on issue to the customer should be destroyed. If there are any cheques or card payments still in circulation, sufficient funds can be left in the account to enable the outstanding cheques and card payments to be paid. If requested, a bank can also transfer the balance of a customer's account to another branch of the bank or to another bank.

In cases where the account has become dormant and the bank is unable to trace the customer, the balance of the account can be transferred to an internal account for dormant accounts or unclaimed balances. This does not mean that the bank appropriates the funds but that the balance of the account will always be available to the customer should they ever arrange to collect it. The *Dormant Bank and Building Society Account Act 2008* allows the government to access funds in dormant accounts and redistribute it to the wider community.

Where the conduct of a bank account has become unsatisfactory and it is desirable from the bank's point of view that the account be closed, this should be done as quickly as possible. A bank will view as unsatisfactory conduct:

- cheques being issued without arrangements being made to enable them to be paid on presentation

- repeated inconvenience to the bank by arrestments or garnishee orders being lodged. Arrestments are used in Scotland with garnishee orders being used in England and Wales. They are orders served on the bank compelling it to hold funds held to the credit of the customer named in the arrestment or garnishee order as attached for the benefit of the party upon whose benefit the arrestment of garnishee order has been lodged.

- any other circumstances which causes the bank embarrassment or inconvenience.

Allowing that the account is to be closed as soon as possible, it has been held in the past that a banker must give reasonable notice of intention to close the account. What constitutes "reasonable" notice would depend on the individual circumstances.

However, the Banking Conduct of Business Sourcebook states that 30 days notice of the intention to close the account should be given to the customer, except in the instance of fraud, threatening or abusive behaviour, etc.

The correct procedure is for the customer to be advised that the bank wants the account to be closed.

So far we have only considered the position when the customer's account is in credit; however, it could be argued that it is more likely that a bank will wish an account to be closed if it is overdrawn, especially if this is without the bank's prior approval. Overdrafts are repayable on demand and in such cases the bank should request the customer to refrain from issuing further cheques or making card payments and to lodge sufficient funds to repay the outstanding overdraft and also enable any outstanding cheques and card payments to be paid.

Where the account is overdrawn and the bank wishes to terminate the relationship, the bank would of course be justified in returning unpaid cheques which would increase an unauthorised overdraft, although the bank would be on dangerous ground if it dishonoured cheques while the customer was operating within an agreed overdraft limit.

Once the bank has advised the customer that the account is to be closed and any lodgements will be placed in permanent reduction of the outstanding debt and sufficient time has been allowed to enable cheques and card payments in the clearing system to be paid within a previously agreed overdraft limit, should the customer advise the bank that they were lodging funds to the account and that these funds have been paid in specifically to cover a cheque that had just been issued by the customer, the bank would not be on safe ground in dishonouring such a cheque. The customer could argue that specific provision had been made to enable the cheque to be paid and that the bank is therefore guilty of wrongful dishonour.

In most cases it would be hoped that the bank and the customer will be able to come to some amicable agreement which could even mean that the bank grants increased facilities to the customer if they can put forward a good enough case on why the bank should continue to support them. In the event of the customer being unwilling to cooperate, then the bank may have to take remedial action.

Death of a customer

A bank has a duty to honour its customers' payments and to permit operations on customers' accounts in terms of the mandate held. On the death of a customer any mandates fall and the bank no longer has any authority to pay items drawn on the account.

Notice of death

Notice of the death of a customer may reach the bank in several ways – perhaps via the notice of death columns in local newspapers, but more commonly by notification by a relative of the deceased or by any other person, although if there is any doubt as to the reliability of the information, the bank should verify the position before taking any action.

Action by the bank

The authority of a bank to pay cheques drawn by a customer ceases as soon as notice of the customer's death is received. This also applied to cheques covered by a cheque guarantee card, or having the customer's debit card number recorded on the reverse and is below the guarantee threshold. The same rule applies for standing orders, direct debits and card payments presented after intimation of the customer's death.

Transactions on the account will normally be stopped, although in some circumstances lodgements will be accepted on the understanding that no sums can be withdrawn from the bank account until the bank receives appropriate instructions.

When information is received as to the legal representatives acting for the deceased customer's representatives, they should be contacted and provided with a note of the balance of the accounts held and information on any other effects of the deceased held by the bank in safe custody.

Administration of the deceased's estate

The balance standing at credit of the bank account, together with all other property owned by the deceased, will form the estate of the deceased. On death, it is usual for whoever is dealing with the estate to ascertain the extent of the estate and to ensure that all debts and obligations are satisfied and the remainder distributed to the entitled parties.

If someone dies leaving a will they are said to have died testate and their estate will be distributed in accordance with the terms of the will. If someone dies intestate, without leaving a will, their estate will be distributed amongst their relatives in accordance with the laws of intestate succession. If no relatives can be traced, the estate will fall to the Crown as *ultimus haeres* (the ultimate heir).

The name given to the person responsible for ingathering and distributing the deceased's estate varies according to the country involved. For ease, we will refer to this person as the "personal representative".

The personal representative will have a document from the necessary authorities which will give them the necessary authority to ingather the deceased's estate and distribute it in accordance with the deceased person's will. The bank should only release funds on sight of this document.

Before making payment, the bank should take a formal note of the following:

- The names and addresses of the personal representatives

- The date upon which the personal representative's authority was issued, along with the issuing body.

- All items held by the bank that are included in the documentation received from the personal representatives. This is because these documents are the authority to uplift these items.

It may be that the estate of a deceased customer is relatively small or that the bank account will form the deceased's entire estate. In such cases, the personal representative may not wish to go to the time or expense of obtaining formal authority to uplift funds and any other assets held by the bank. Depending on the balance of the account, the bank may be prepared to release the funds to the personal representative against their discharge and guarantee or discharge and indemnity. The terms of these is an undertaking from the personal representatives to the bank to repay the funds paid over should a claim be made to the bank at a later date from a party claiming to be the rightful owner of the funds.

In the case of a customer dying intestate, the bank may consider paying the funds to a surviving spouse or all of the surviving children against a discharge and guarantee/indemnity.

When an account is overdrawn

Once again no items should be honoured after the bank is aware of the customer's death. As soon as the name and address of the legal representatives acting in the winding up of the estate is known, they should be provided with a note of the sums due to the bank. The legal representatives should also be provided with a note of any outstanding interest, the rate of interest being charged and should be advised that interest will continue to accrue on the overdraft until it is repaid.

Control of accounts

Before an account is opened, as much information as possible should be obtained about the customer, but this is not enough – how the account is developing should be an ongoing process. Not only will this allow for opportunities of matching relevant products to the customer's needs, but will also ensure that the operation of the account and the use of borrowing facilities does not get out of line with the arrangements agreed at the beginning. Close monitoring of an account should also provide early warning signs that a customer may be in financial difficulty.

Those members of staff in the bank who have the authority to lend funds to customers will have a maximum amount that they can lend without reference to a higher authority. This is called a lending limit. The level of this limit for any member of staff may be determined by:

- the credit scoring facilities available

- the type and value of security offered by the customer

- the experience and competence of the member of staff.

Most banks will have a centralised unit that deals with the sanctioning of credit and the control of lending for larger customers. However, it is also common to find that lending and control also happens at a local level for smaller loans and packaged lending. This section on the control of lending will only consider what happens at this local level.

Sources of information

Customers provide banks with a great deal of information about their lifestyles and financial circumstances, often without realising it:

- Card payments – looking at the beneficiaries of card payments will inform you how a customer is spending his/her (or the bank's!) money; a large payment by card or cheque can indicate a large purchase by the customer; also payments for round amounts may indicate that the customer is making payments to account with another credit provider.

- Standing orders and direct debits – these will give you a good idea of a customer's regular commitments; a standing order to a finance company could indicate a deterioration in the customer's financial circumstances or possibly a lost selling opportunity for the bank; an increase in the amount of the monthly standing order to a building society could mean that the customer has moved house or obtained a top-up mortgage or capital release loan.

- Credits to the account – is the customer's salary mandated to the bank? If so, the name of the customer's employer (although this should already be known from the opening of the account) and the current level of his/her salary will be known. If credits of this nature were to suddenly stop, the customer may have lost their job.

- Discussions with the customer – these can take place at meetings between the bank and the customer or during the course of an informal conversation over the counter when the customer calls into the bank.

- Conduct of the bank account generally – what use is being made of overdraft facilities? Are there signs that the customer is living outwith their means or is in financial difficulty? If the overdraft balance exceeds the amount of salary, then hard core borrowing could develop. Hard core borrowing is the expression used to describe the situation where a customer has an overdraft facility on their account, but the account never swings into credit. For example, an overdraft limit may be £5,000, but the lowest level of the debit balance on this account is £1,250. In this case, the hard core borrowing is "1,250. This can be a sign that the customer is living beyond their means.

- Arrestments/garnishee orders – these can be a sign that the customer is experiencing financial difficulty.

- Annual accounts and cash flow forecasts – information about the business customer's financial position.

Daily report on overdrawn balances

This is a key daily monitoring tool used to monitor customers' accounts. The form and content of the report may vary from bank to bank but the following example will give a rough idea of the information that can normally be found in the report:

Daily Report for Northtown Branch						23 May 20XX
A/C No	Name	Bal	Limit	Excess	Fwd Post	Last moved
112748264	Wilson J & M	£2507dr	£2500	£7	£45	21/5
122441153	Walker I	£4500dr	£4750			3/1
162337649	Jackson J & J	£5993dr	£6000			22/5
253661182	Browns Limited	£8572dr	£8000	£572	£250	19/5
152263094	Stewart J & A	£4657dr	£4500	£157		21/4

In this case the customers are operating within their limit and would not normally be a cause for concern, but the credit limit is under some pressure. Further investigation may be required here to ascertain whether there are fluctuations in the account and if it swings into credit from time to time or if there is a significant "hard core" element of the overdraft.

The balance of this account is well within the agreed limit, but it is of some concern that the account has not moved for almost six months. Why have there been no credits to the account? Has the customer ceased trading or is he an individual who has lost his job? Remedial action may be necessary here to avoid loss to the bank and this account may be referred to the department dealing with collections and recoveries.

It's not possible to determine whether or not the cheques should be paid from the limited information available and further investigation is required. In the case of Mr and Mrs Wilson, they are at present only £7 over their limit and if the forward posted items are paid, the excess would increase to £52. The bank may be prepared to pay the cheques although it may also consider contacting the customers requesting that funds be lodged to the account as soon as possible as the bank cannot guarantee that it will pay any further cheques issued.

The situation with Browns Limited is slightly different as the amount of the facilities, the over-limit position and the amount of cheques presented are all significantly greater than in the case of the Wilsons. You may consider that the cheques should be returned unpaid which would of course have an adverse effect on the business in the eyes of its suppliers who may then take action to recover sums due to them. Alternatively they may refuse to make any further supplies to the company unless on "cash on delivery" terms which could seriously affect the future of the business.

Obviously it is essential to consider who the payees of the cheques are. Supposing the business operates from leased premises, what would happen if the bank refused to pay a cheque to the company's landlord in respect of the rental? However, if the cheques are retained at the bank's central processing unit, it may take time to ascertain the names of the payees of individual cheques.

There is a £157 excess on the account but no cheques have been presented today. The account has not moved for over a month. Were the cheques which created the excess paid on the understanding that funds would be lodged within a few days or weeks? Perhaps it is time to contact the customers and find out what their proposals are for reducing the overdraft to within the agreed limit.

Formal reviews

In accordance with normal banking practice, overdrafts are repayable on demand, but it is usual for overdraft facilities to be granted subject to annual review on the strict understanding, of course, that the bank can call for repayment at any time. It is customary to review facilities regularly to:

- check whether or not the facilities at the current level are still required

- check that the customer has not been misusing the facilities

- compare the account history with the projections provided at the time the facility was approved or last renewed.

The review will normally involve a meeting between the bank and the customer at which the continued need for the facilities will be discussed. If the customer is in business, the annual review will normally coincide with the production of the customer's balance sheet and profit and loss account.

Analysis of financial statements is a specialist skill and will not be covered in this course. The banker, however, can compare the level of profit made with the profit that the customer predicted that would be made. If the customer has not made any profit but incurred a loss, the reasons for this should be ascertained and action taken by the customer to ensure that no further losses are incurred. At the end of the review meeting, the banker – if satisfied with the proposals discussed – will usually renew the facilities for a further period.

Remedial action

Sadly, there will be occasions where, despite every effort being made by the bank to monitor accounts and keep borrowing within agreed limits or have borrowing repaid in accordance with the agreed repayment programme, the bank will have no alternative other than to take remedial action to obtain repayment of the facilities and prevent or minimise loss to the bank.

The bank will normally call for immediate repayment of the facilities within a given timescale, say 7 or 10 days. It is unlikely that the customer will be able to make full repayment within that time and the bank will probably accept a substantial payment to account together with acceptable proposals for repayment of the remaining sum.

At this point it should be noted that if the borrowing is in the name of individuals, clubs, partnerships with either 2 or 3 partners, or business lending under £25,000, then the borrowing is subject to the terms of the Consumer Credit Acts, 1974 and 2006. Assuming that no opt outs have been made by the borrower, strict procedures require to be followed by the bank if it wishes to take action to recover sums due. If calling up notices or default notices (in terms of the *Consumer Credit Acts*) do not elicit the desired response, the bank will probably refer the position to a central department responsible for the recovery of advances.

Collections and recoveries departments

Collections will occur earlier on in the process of managing irregular (or, as they are often called, delinquent) accounts. The aim of the collections process is to bring the account back onto a regular footing, whilst preserving the long term relationship with the customer. Most banks will conduct their collections activities in-house, rather than by outsourcing them. Often a bank will look at its collections operation as an extension of its customer services function.

Recoveries, on the other hand, will deal with irregular accounts after collections have concluded their activities with these customers and the account is still irregular. The aim of a recoveries department is to collect the debt whilst severing the relationship with the customer. Recoveries actions usually involve third parties, perhaps by the use of external debt collection agencies, or through use of the courts.

There is a statutory requirement for a default notice to be sent to a customer before payment of the full outstanding balance can be demanded. This default notice is a key action at the end of the collections and the start of the recoveries phases.

The default notice is issued first and is an explanation to the customer that they have breached the terms of the agreement. The call up notice comes after the default notice and is issued only when the bank is holding security. The purpose of the call up notice is to call up the security – not the debt, therefore, if a customer has not given the bank security, they would only receive a default notice. Prescribed documentation is used as a result of the Consumer Credit Act 2006.

How an account may become irregular

There are several reasons why a customer's account may become irregular. In the majority of cases, these are brought about by a change in the customer's circumstances and/or an inability on the customer's part to manage their finances.

Examples

- Loss of job, marital breakdown or illness – these can disrupt the customer's lifestyle and also result in a loss of income. The combination of these circumstances may result in short or long term payment problems.

- Missed payments due to, say, an oversight or the customer being away on holiday or business. In the majority of these cases, the

> customer will make the payment within a month and will rarely have contact with the collections department.
>
> • Incorrect set up of direct debit resulting in a payment not being made by the due date.
>
> • Disputes with the bank – the customer decides to withhold payment and may continue to do so until the dispute has been resolved.
>
> • The customer is living beyond their means

No matter the cause, if the customer's account has become irregular, it will soon be referred to the collections department.

Options to recover debt

A number of options are open to a bank to obtain recovery of a "doubtful" debt.

If the bank holds security for the obligations of the customer, it can take steps to realise the security which could involve evicting the customer from their house and selling it to repay bank borrowing, or surrendering a life policy which the customer has given the bank as security. This is obviously a very serious course of action which would normally only be taken by the bank in extreme circumstances and after a great deal of thought.

The bank could also refer the matter to their legal representatives or to a specialist debt recovery agency that can pursue the debt on behalf of the bank – with court action being one possible tactic.

The bank could also arrange to lodge an arrestment/garnishee order in the hands of any party which owes money to the customer. This will have the effect of preventing the customer access to the monies which will be attached to the order of the bank. The bank may be aware, for example, that the customer has a savings account with another bank or a building society and an arrestment/garnishee order lodged in the hands of the other bank or building society would prevent the customer from withdrawing the funds and, on completion of further action, would enable the funds to be remitted to the bank in repayment or reduction of the customer's debt. In view of the nature of this type of action it is common for arrestment/

garnishee order to be lodged in the hands of banks seeking to attach funds due by them to their customers.

In the case of a limited company, the bank can seek to put the company into liquidation. A liquidator will be appointed who will take control of all the company's assets. The liquidator will attempt to sell off assets and the proceeds will be distributed by way of a dividend to all the company's creditors. In the event of the assets of the company being insufficient to repay each creditor the full amount owing, the dividend will be scaled down to a pro rata share of the sum due and will be expressed as so much per pound.

Example

If it were 75p per £, and the bank were owed £10,000 by the company, it would receive £7,500. Unless it held directors' guarantees, the bank would probably have to write off the remainder of the debt.

If the bank held a bond and floating charge, it could appoint a receiver to administer the company's affairs. Receivership is a complex process the details of which are not included here, but it is worthwhile remembering that while a liquidator acts in the best interests of all the creditors of a company, a receiver looks after the interests of the bond and floating chargeholder only. This is one of many good reasons for taking a bond and floating charge from a company.

Operations on customer's current accounts involves work and expense for the bank and the bank is entitled to make a charge to cover staff costs as well as the costs of providing cheque books and other items of stationery, plastic cards, etc. In the past, the charge for personal customers was based around the number and type of transactions passing through the account during a charging period; however, it is now common for a fixed fee to be levied to accounts that are liable for service charge. Banks may also make a charge on each occasion that it is necessary to write to a customer informing them that their bank account is not being operated in accordance with the agreed arrangements and requesting that corrective action be taken.

At present, most banks do not make any charge as long as current accounts remain in credit for the charging period although, provided that sufficient notice was given to customers, this arrangement could end. It would then be open to banks to levy service charges even if the account remains in credit or to raise the minimum balance required to enjoy "free" banking.

In the case of businesses, charging per debit item may not adequately remunerate the bank as a great deal of the work involved in maintaining the account may be counting cash lodgements paid in at the counter. In such cases the service charge will usually be calculated based on the number and type of transactions passing through the account.

For example, if there is a high volume of cash transactions, the charge will normally be higher than if most of the transactions through the account are electronic – and thus cheaper for the bank. It is also possible for a business to negotiate a fixed service charge fee in advance, based on the estimated activity on the account. This charge will be applied to the account each month.

At present, most banks will not charge a new business during its first year of operation. Others may extend this concession further; for example, only charging 50% of the service charge during the second year of operation. Some banks offer a "free business banking for life" service which operates by putting a ceiling on the amount of transactions passing through the account on a monthly basis; for example, £3,000 cash and 150 items. Provided the business customer operates within these parameters, the bank promises not to levy service charges. There are sometimes other conditions associated with this – for example, lodgements may only be made by way of a drop box or automated deposit machine, as opposed to over the counter.

It is a requirement of the Banking Conduct of Business rules that the level of bank charges is communicated to customers and not increased without reasonable notice being given to the customer. It is therefore usual for a bank to write to a customer advising them of the charges that will apply to their account and how the charges will be calculated. Once such a letter has been issued, the bank will not be able to increase the level of charges until the term of the letter expires.

In addition to service charges for the day-to-day operation of current accounts, banks will also charge an arrangement fee to remunerate the bank and cover the costs involved in arranging and agreeing a loan.

Adults with incapacity

There may come a time when, because a person is incapable of managing their property and financial affairs or personal welfare, they will need someone to do this for them. A friend, relative or professional may then be appointed to hold a lasting power of attorney allowing them to act on that individual's behalf. A power of attorney is a legal document that allows an individual to appoint someone they trust as an attorney to make decisions on that person's behalf.

Legislation exists to provide ways in which it is possible to safeguard the welfare and finances of adults who do not have the capacity to make some or all decisions on behalf of themselves, due either to a mental disorder or an inability to communicate. As a result, other people are empowered to make decisions on behalf of the incapacitated person and also allows capable individuals to make provision for another person or persons to make decisions on their behalf in the potential event of them losing their capacity at some point in the future.

There are several ways in which decisions or actions can be taken on behalf of an incapacitated adult. These interventions may cover property or financial affairs or personal welfare matters, including healthcare. When deciding whether to intervene, the following principles must be applied:

- the intervention must be necessary and must benefit the adult

- the intervention must be the minimum necessary to achieve the purpose

- the person's present and past wishes and feelings must be taken into account

- the views of the adult's nearest relative and primary carer and any other person with the power to intervene in the adult's affairs or personal welfare must be taken into account.

- the adult should be encouraged to use any skills that he or she has.

Capable adults may arrange for their welfare to be safeguarded and for their affairs to be managed in the future should they lose their capability. This is done by giving another person – who could be a relative, a carer, a professional person, or a trusted friend – power of attorney to look after some or all of their property and financial affairs. This may extend to making specified decisions about the adult's personal welfare, including medical treatment.

All continuing and welfare powers of attorney must be registered with the Public Guardian in order to be effective. Individuals – usually relatives or carers – can apply to the Public Guardian to gain access to the funds of an adult who is incapable of managing them. Authorised care establishments can also manage a limited amount of the funds and property of those residents who are not able to do so themselves.

A local authority or any person claiming an interest in the adult's affairs may make applications for interventions or guardianship orders.

Question   **4**

Go to question section starting on page 243

Check with the answer at the back of the book.

Review

Now consider the main learning points which were introduced in this chapter.

Go through them and tick each one when you are happy that you fully understand each point.

Then check back to the objectives at the beginning of the chapter and match them to the learning points.

Reread any section you are unsure of before moving on.

When a new account is opened, the banker should obtain as much information as possible about the customer. This information should be updated throughout the life of the account.

☐

An account may be closed if it has become dormant, if the customer wishes to close the account or if the bank gives notice that it wishes the account to be closed.

☐

A bank has a duty to honour its customers' cheques and to permit operations on customers' accounts in terms of the mandate held. On the death of a customer any mandates fall and the bank no longer has any authority to pay cheques drawn on the account.

☐

By close monitoring of an account, any early warning signs that a customer is in financial difficulty should soon become apparent.

☐

The aim of the collections process in managing irregular accounts is to bring the account back on to a regular footing, whilst preserving the long term relationship with the customer.

☐

Recoveries deal with irregular accounts after collections have concluded their activities and the account is still irregular. The aim of a recoveries department is to collect the debt whilst severing the relationship with the customer.

☐

Operations on customer's current accounts involve work and expense for the bank and the bank is entitled to make a charge for its services.

☐

 Key words in this chapter are given below. There is space to write your own revision notes and to add any other words or phrases that you want to remember.

customer profiling

nova debita

arrestment

testate

intestate

ultimus haeres

default notice

collections and recoveries

garnishee order

personal representatives

due diligence

Multiple choice questions   4

Try these self-test questions to assess your understanding of what you have read in this chapter.
The answers are at the back of the book.

1   The term used to describe the information gathering carried out by a bank on either a new customer or a borrowing customer is:

   A   Researching

   B   Due diligence

   C   Confirming

   D   Gleaning

2   Which one of the following would NOT fall under the Consumer Credit Acts 1974 and 2006?

   A   A personal loan for £20,000

   B   A business loan for £20,000

   C   A business loan for £60,000

   D   A personal loan for £60,000

3   Kenneth has a loan with ABC Bank, set up as a regulated loan under the provisions of the Consumer Credit Acts 1974 and 2006. The Bank has decided that there is no prospect that Kenneth can repay the debt. In this instance it will issue which one of the following?

   A   an arrestment

   B   a default notice

   C   a calling up order

   D   a calling in order

Multiple choice questions   **4**

4   The primary responsibility of a liquidator is to which one of the following?

A   the company in liquidation

B   the creditors of the company in liquidation

C   the trustee

D   the shareholders of the company in liquidation

5   A bank's collections department seeks to:

A   Realise any security and apply the proceeds in permanent reduction of the debt

B   Recover the sums due to the bank and close the account

C   Recover the sums due to the bank and maintain the relationship with the customer

D   Issue the relevant call up notices to defaulting customers

6   Which one of the following is not a purpose of a formal review of a customer's overdraft facility?

A   to determine whether the facility is still required

B   to check that the customer has not been misusing the facility

C   to compare the account history with projected future performance

D   to identify actions that will reduce the overdraft as soon as possible

Multiple choice questions   **4**

7   The term *ultimus haeres* refers to which one of the following?

A   the next-of-kin of a deceased person

B   the executor-dative appointed in respect of the estate of a deceased person

C   the right of the state to the estate of a deceased person if no relatives are traced

D   the ultimate beneficiary of a will of a deceased person

8   What is the position in respect of cheques written but not cleared immediately before the death of an account holder?

A   they can be processed in the normal manner

B   they can be processed once the estate is confirmed

C   the cheques must be processed but marked "deceased"

D   they must be returned unpaid

9   If an account is classified as *nova debita*, what does this mean?

A   withdrawals are classed as "new debt" when a partner is retiring

B   the overdraft limit has been revised

C   the borrower's total borrowings have been consolidated

D   the debit balance on the account of a deceased person has been confirmed

5 Cheques

Objectives

By the end of this chapter, you should be able to:

- Explain what a cheque is.

- Describe the parties to a cheque.

- State what is meant by "Funds Attached".

- Describe the significance of a crossing on a cheque.

- Define "truncation".

- Explain the roles of the paying and the collecting banker.

Introduction

We looked briefly at cheques when we studied the main features of a current account. As you will be aware, the use of personal cheques has diminished greatly in recent years, but as cheques play such an important part in banking we will spend this whole chapter looking at exactly what a cheque is, how a cheque is transferred between parties and how it finds its way from the person in whose favour it was issued to the bank account on which it was drawn. The use of cheques by personal customers has greatly diminished in recent years as people have found other ways to transmit money – for example, through the use of plastic cards and online banking. However, cheques are still used by some personal customers and also by many business customers.

A bank has two roles in the cheque process: customers pay into their bank accounts cheques which require to be presented to the bank where the account of the person who issued the cheque is held and the bank has to pay cheques when they are presented by other banks. Thus we'll be examining the roles of the collecting banker and the paying banker.

What is a cheque?

A cheque is a document which conveys to a bank an order from one of its customers to pay money to a third party or to the customer if they wish to draw cash. A cheque is a bill of exchange, therefore much of the law relating to cheques is set out in the *Bills of Exchange Act 1882*. You will not need to study bills of exchange other than cheques for this course. Basically, a bill of exchange is an order to pay money; they have been used as a means of transacting business for hundreds of years. The *1882 Act* was supplemented by the *Cheques Act 1957* and the *Cheques Act 1992*. By using the definitions in these Acts we have the following detailed definition of a cheque:

> **"A cheque is an unconditional order in writing drawn by one party on another, who must be a banker, signed by the drawer, requiring the banker to pay on demand a sum certain in money to or to the order of a specified person or to bearer."**

This definition is useful in emphasising the main features of a cheque and the essentials to which a cheque must conform. There are normally three parties to a cheque:

- the person who issues the cheque and whose bank account will be debited when the cheque is paid is called the drawer

- the party to whom the cheque is addressed, who must be a banker

- the party in whose favour the cheque is payable and to whom the money is to be paid is called the payee.

Some of the essential features of a cheque are:

- It must contain an order to pay and the order must be unconditional as far as the banker is concerned; for example, it would not be appropriate for a bank to be faced with an order to pay someone £250 "if he has finished decorating my house" or "if she is wearing a green dress".

- It must be in writing. Banks issue standard forms of cheques which are completed by customers. It is not unlawful for a cheque to be written in pencil but banks tend to actively discourage this practice as they can be easily altered by erasing and amending either the payee, the amount or both. Businesses which issue large numbers of cheques may have the cheques including the name of the payee, the amount and the "signature" printed by computer which is permissible, although in such cases the customer will normally be expected to grant an indemnity to the bank as a means of protection should the bank pay a cheque, the issue of which was not authorised by the customer.

- It must be drawn for a sum certain in money. The sum may be expressed either in words or in figures, although in practice, and as a means of preventing fraud and removing any doubt in cases where the drawer's writing is not clear, the amount of a cheque requires to be written in words and figures. Where the amount in words differs from the amount in figures, the bank will normally return the cheque unpaid marked "Amounts Differ".

- The amount must be payable on demand, that is it is not permissible for a cheque to be issued requesting the bank to pay in 30 days time. (There is of course nothing to stop someone from dating a cheque in the future – we'll look at post dated cheques later.)

- A cheque must be payable to or to the order of a specified person.

The drawer

In order to be valid, a cheque must be signed by the drawer, although the signature may be lithographed by machine or computer. If a customer's signature on a cheque is forged, the bank is not entitled to debit the customer's account. If a bank does pay such a cheque, the customer must be reimbursed, no matter how skilfully the signature has been forged.

The drawer should act responsibly when issuing cheques and take care to ensure that cheques are drawn in a clear manner and that all reasonable steps have been taken to reduce the opportunity for fraudulent alterations by third parties.

The customer can assist the banks in their fight against crime by writing their cheques in a responsible manner. If a cheque is written in block capitals in ballpoint pen it is more difficult to alter than, say, a cheque written in fibre tip pen, especially if the standard of handwriting lends itself to alteration. The customer should also take care not to leave spaces between any words or figures on the cheque. A customer may issue a cheque for:

£100   ONE HUNDRED   POUNDS

but if the cheque is not completed in a responsible manner, it may not be too difficult for some dishonest person to alter the cheque to:

£100,000 ONE HUNDRED THOUSAND POUNDS

Case study

London Joint Stock Bank -v- Macmillan and Arthur, 1918

This case established the principle that if a customer is careless in the manner in which they draw a cheque and fraudulent alteration of the cheque is facilitated, then it is the customer and not the bank that should bear any loss.

Obviously it is important that when a customer issues a cheque, they should ensure that there are funds in the bank account or that an authorised overdraft has been agreed to enable the cheque to be paid when it is presented for payment.

The payee

A cheque may be made payable to or to the order of a specified person or to bearer. Where the cheque is not payable to bearer, the payee must be named. A cheque may be payable to two or more persons jointly or to one person of two or more, for example James or Fiona Smith; or to one or some of several payees, for example any two of James and Fiona Smith, William George, John and Anne Rutherford or Gordon Johnstone; or to the holder of an office, for example the treasurer of Edinburgh Kayaking Club.

Cheques are sometimes drawn payable to "Cash" or "Wages" and are generally looked upon as being payable to bearer.

Date

In practice all cheques are dated when they are issued, but in terms of the *Bills of Exchange Act*, a cheque is still valid even if it is undated. Any person in lawful possession of a cheque which is incomplete in any material particular may fill in any omission (except the signature). If the bank is presented with a cheque for payment and the cheque is undated, in terms of the law, the bank may insert the date but in practice banks refuse to pay cheques that have not been dated by the drawer. The banks' view is that although the drawer may have signed the cheque, he may not have intended that it should be issued and paid.

A cheque is valid even although it is post dated, that is it bears a date later than the date of issue; however, the bank on which a post dated cheque is drawn should decline to honour the cheque until the date stated on the cheque. It could be the case that the drawer of the cheque dies or is declared bankrupt or places a stop on the cheque before the date stated on the cheque. If that bank had already paid the cheque it may be necessary to reimburse the customer, therefore this is an area which requires care.

A cheque can be regarded as stale if it has been in circulation for what is considered an unreasonably long time. What constitutes a reasonable time has not been legally challenged, but the practice of bankers is to regard cheques more than six months old as being stale and to obtain the confirmation of the drawer prior to making payment. Alternatively, the banker may return the cheque unpaid, marked "Out of date".

Alterations on cheques

Any alteration to a cheque must be made with the consent of the drawer who should either sign or initial at each point on the cheque where an alteration has been made. Where there are two or more drawers, they must all authorise the alteration by signing/initialling at the appropriate place on the cheque.

If a bank pays a cheque which has been materially altered, it may be necessary to reimburse the customer if the alterations have not been authenticated. Similarly, where a cheque has been torn into pieces and pasted back together again it would not be advisable to pay the cheque without obtaining the confirmation of the drawer as they may have intended to cancel it.

A negotiable instrument

A cheque is a negotiable instrument which means that it can be negotiated for value and may be passed from one party to another and that it is a useful method of settling business transactions. An important feature of a negotiable instrument is that when it is transferred, title to the instrument passes from hand to hand by delivery. Instruments which are merely transferable, for example a share certificate, need some other form of document executed – in the case of a share certificate a stock transfer form – or some other process before title is actually transferred.

As you will see when you study the section of this chapter on cheque crossings, it is now very unusual for cheques to be passed from one person to another in this way. There is, however, one exception to this.

The exception we are looking at here is the services provided by some organisations in the high street who, amongst other things, offer a cheque cashing service. An example of this type of organisation is "Cash Converters" who will cash third party cheques for people who do not have a bank account. There is, of course, a charge for this service.

Other examples of negotiable instruments are bearer bonds, promissory notes, other types of bills of exchange and, of course, bank notes. A cheque is negotiable because, by the simple act of indorsing it and handing it over, the payee can transfer to someone else the right to receive the amount stated in the cheque. We will also consider crossed cheques and the terms of the *Cheques Act 1992* which restrict the ability of a cheque to be transferable and therefore to be a negotiable instrument.

Crossed cheques

There are only two types of crossings authorised by the *Bills of Exchange Act 1882*: general crossings and special crossings.

General crossings

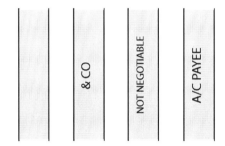

Special crossings

A crossing is basically a direction to the bank placed on the face of the cheque by the drawer that the amount should be paid only to a banker or through a bank account. There was nothing in the *Bills of Exchange Act* or the *Cheques Act 1957* which prevented a banker from paying a crossed cheque in cash over the counter, but in such circumstances the banker would be accountable to the true owner of the cheque should the wrong person have been paid.

However, the *Cheques Act 1992* amended both the *Bills of Exchange Act* and the *1957 Cheques Act* and made all crossed cheques non-transferable. This altered the legal position of cheques crossed "Account Payee" (which until then had no statutory authority and did not affect the transferability of a cheque) and provided a statutory framework within which banks could deal with non-transferable cheques. The *1992 Act* also provided more protection to the public by ensuring that such cheques can only be paid to the payee named on the cheque.

Prior to the *1992 Act*, banks generally discouraged the use of non-transferable cheques in view of what was seen as the practical difficulties in handling them. A cheque would be non-transferable if the words "or order," generally preprinted on a cheque, had been struck out and initialled by the drawer. The words "not transferable" could also be written across the face of the cheque. A cheque so drawn could only be paid to the payee specified, and if there is evidence of its having been transferred, the banker on whom it was drawn should decline payment.

Cheques were generally regarded as negotiable instruments and the drawing of cheques in non-transferable form was greatly discouraged by banks. Some banks even had a policy of not permitting their customers to issue such cheques, as non-transferable cheques placed upon the bank the burden of enquiry as to whether the correct person was being paid. The *Cheques Act 1992* had the effect of making the following cheques non-transferable which means that they cannot be accepted for credit for the account of anyone other than the named payee nor should cash be paid to any third party. Such cheques should only be paid into a bank account in name of the payee of the cheque:

- cheques payable to a named payee followed by the word "only"

- cheques payable to a named payee and marked "non-transferable"

- uncrossed cheques payable to a named payee and marked "not negotiable"

- cheques marked "Account payee" or "Account payee only"

- cheques bearing wording clearly intended to ensure that they are payable to the named payee and to no other party.

Most cheques are now issued with a preprinted account payee crossing making them non-transferable, eliminating the capability of such cheques to be negotiated so there should be fewer problems for bankers in dealing with cheques.

When a cheque bears an "account payee" crossing, there is no longer any need to combine it with a "not negotiable" crossing as the "not negotiable" crossing is relevant only on a cheque payable to "or order", that is one which is transferable.

On cheques where there is an "account payee" crossing, no endorsement is possible to allow for transferring the cheque as such cheques are non-transferable.

Truncation

The Deregulation (Bills of Exchange) order 1996 served to: This Order:

- amended the *1882 Act* to permit notice of dishonour of bills of exchange generally to be given by facsimile transmission or other electronic means

- inserted a new provision into the *1882 Act* to allow cheques to be presented for payment at an address specified by the paying bank in the *London* and *Edinburgh Gazettes*

- inserted a new provision in the *1882 Act* to enable cheques to be presented for payment by notification of their essential features by electronic means rather than the actual cheque being physically presented

- amended the *1957 Act* to allow a certified copy of an unendorsed cheque to be accepted as evidence of receipt of payment.

For truncation of cheques, the third point above is important. Until the *1996 Order* came into force, the *1882 Act* required that cheques drawn on a particular branch of a bank be returned to that branch for payment (if the branch address is printed on the cheque).

Some banks had a central address printed on the cheque and therefore the cheques had to be presented to that address for payment. Because the clearing of cheques has now reached the stage where all the essential details of the cheque are recorded electronically – the serial number, the drawer's account number, sorting code of the branch, and the collecting bank adds the amount of the cheque – banks have been exchanging this data electronically as part of the clearing process.

The full benefit of the electronic exchange of data can only be achieved by truncation of the cheques, which is the removal of the obligation to send cheques back to the relevant branch of the paying bank. When a cheque is truncated it is retained at some point in the clearing process. This can be either at the collecting branch, or at a central point within the paying bank.

The second point above permits an alternative place for physical presentation of the cheque if the truncation route is not taken. It means that the paying bank can pay the cheque if it is physically presented to the address which they have published in the *Gazettes* even if it is not the one printed on the cheque. The important point to note is that it does not enable the holders of the cheques to demand payment at any branch of the paying bank.

As a safeguard, if a truncated cheque's details have been received electronically by the paying bank, that bank, not later than the business day following receipt of notification of the electronic details, may request that the cheque be physically presented. This has the immediate effect of rendering void the electronic presentment of the cheque details.

The role of the paying banker

In the cheque process a bank can play two roles – the paying banker and the collecting banker. When a customer issues a cheque as a means of settling a payment due, provided sufficient funds are in the account or the customer has agreed an overdraft facility with the bank, the customer will expect the cheque to be paid when it is presented to the bank. Certainly the payee of the cheque will expect payment, especially if goods or services have already been provided to the customer.

In the event therefore of the cheque being returned unpaid, the customer will be placed in an extremely embarrassing position with the payee of the cheque and so it is essential that the bank does not wrongfully dishonour a cheque. If this is done without justification, the banker may be liable for breach of contract and have to pay damages for injury to the customer's credit. In the past, it was deemed that these damages would be greater for a business customer than for a personal customer, but the following case changed this.

Case study

Kpoharor -v- Woolwich Building Society, 1995

In this case it was held by the English Court of Appeal that circumstances had changed since the earlier rule had been formulated. History had changed the social factors which moulded the rule in the nineteenth century. It was not only a tradesman of whom it could be said that refusal to meet his cheque was "so obviously injurious to his credit" that he should "recover, without allegations of special damage, reasonable compensation for the injury done to his credit". The credit rating of individuals was as important for their personal transactions, including mortgages and hire purchase as well as banking facilities, as it was for those who were engaged in trade.

In the court's view there is a presumption of some damage in every case and is not limited to a business or trading context, and so in future cases it is likely that a personal customer whose cheque is wrongfully dishonoured may be able to claim substantial damages without having to prove a special damage which hitherto would have been necessary.

If the bank is at fault in this way, a letter of apology should be sent to the customer, the account should be corrected, and the payee should be advised that if the cheque is re-presented it will be paid, and that no fault at all lies with the customer. This may help to reduce damages if the customer brings a civil action.

It is the duty of a banker to honour customer's cheques provided that:

- there are sufficient funds in the customer's account with the bank or a suitable overdraft limit has been agreed

- the cheques have been drawn correctly and have been signed by the customer

- there is no legal reason prohibiting payment.

Are there funds available to enable a cheque to be paid?

The banker must exercise great care to ensure that there are customer's funds available for payment of a cheque that has been presented. In cases where the customer only maintains one account with the bank, the position is obviously a very simple case of checking to see that the balance on the account, or the unused portion of an agreed overdraft, is at least equal to the amount of the cheque. A check should be made, of course, that all entries to the customer's account have been processed and that the balance on the account is therefore correct.

Funds may have been paid into the customer's account by bank giro credit at another branch of the bank or at another bank. If the bank dishonours a customer's cheque before becoming aware that funds have been paid in via this method, it will not be liable for damages, unless of course this was as a result of the bank's negligence or an error by the branch in processing the credit entry.

Prohibiting payment of a cheque

Section 75 of the *Bills of Exchange Act 1882* recognises two circumstances when a bank will legally be prohibited from making payment of a cheque:

- countermand of payment by the drawer

- notice of the customer's death.

Countermand of payment or a customer's instruction to "stop" payment of a cheque should be communicated to the bank in writing. The drawer of the cheque should provide the bank with sufficient information for the cheque to be identified and stopped. The serial number of a cheque has been held in court to be the one certain means of identifying a cheque.

Example

If a bank pays a cheque after its authority to do so has been countermanded by the customer, the bank will not be entitled to debit the customer's account, but if the bank were requested to stop payment on cheque number 0023415 for £125 payable to J Smith and the correct serial number of the cheque was 0023416, the bank may be entitled to assume that cheque number 0023416 was issued as a replacement for cheque number 0023415 which was perhaps lost or stolen and would not be liable if cheque number 0023416 were paid. This is a fairly frequent occurrence when the bank is asked to countermand a cheque.

When a cheque is drawn by one party to a joint account, payment may be stopped by the other party. Similarly, if a cheque has been issued by a firm or a limited company and has been signed by one partner or director, payment may be stopped by any partner or director or in fact any signatory to the account.

If a cheque is presented to the bank for payment through the clearing system the banker has until close of business that day to decide whether or not the cheque will be paid. The customer can therefore countermand payment of a cheque that is already with the banker if payment is countermanded at some time before close of business on the day on which the cheque is presented to the banker through the clearing system.

A final point to note here is that if a banker pays a cheque, payment of which has been countermanded by the drawer, not only will he be unable to debit the customer's account, but also will be unable to recover the amount involved from the person who received payment unless this person did not act in good faith. In such circumstances, the onus would be on the bank to prove that the payee or holder of the cheque did not act in good faith.

As discussed in the previous chapter, notice of a customer's death terminates a banker's authority to pay the customer's cheques. The notice may be from one of the relatives of the deceased or from any other reliable source, including intimation in a newspaper. Cheques issued by a company and signed by a director are not affected by the death of the director. Similarly, cheques issued by a firm and signed by a partner can still be paid notwithstanding the death of the partner that has signed the cheque.

There are other reasons for terminating a banker's authority to pay cheques including:

- notice that the customer has been declared bankrupt, or in the case of a limited company, notice that it is to be wound up or is to have a liquidator, receiver, administrator or administrative receiver appointed

- the customer's insanity – formal declaration by a qualified person and the appointment of someone to look after the affairs of the insane person (not the banker's personal opinion)

- knowledge of any defect in title of the person presenting the cheque for payment.

The lodging of an arrestment or garnishee order in the hands of a banker will not terminate the authority to pay the customer's cheques, but the customer's account will be frozen and the banker will be unable to pay cheques unless they are willing to grant the customer an overdraft facility.

Forgery of the drawer's signature

Where the customer's signature has been forged on a cheque, the banker cannot debit the account if the cheque is paid. You will remember that a cheque is an unconditional order in writing drawn by one person on another, who must be a banker, signed by the drawer.

If the customer's signature has been forged, the cheque is not the customer's genuine order in writing. The fact that the forgery may be very skilfully done and that it is almost impossible to tell the forged signature from the genuine signature provides no comfort. The banker may not be liable if the customer is aware that their signature is being forged but takes no action to inform the bank and possibly enables the bank to avoid future loss. This is highlighted in the following case.

Case study

Greenwood -v- Martins Bank Limited, 1931

The wife of a customer forged cheques on his account. She subsequently confessed to her husband, who took no action until after her death. He then sued the bank to recover the money paid but was unsuccessful as the judge in the case took the view that it was the customer's duty to inform the bank of the forgery as soon as he knew of it.

The role of the collecting banker

Bankers are also asked to collect cheques for their customers. In many cases the cheques will not be drawn on the bank but on other banks or perhaps other branches of the same bank. When the bank accepts such cheques from its customers it takes on the role of the collecting banker.

When collecting cheques for one of its customers, the bank is exposed to the danger that it may collect and receive payment for a cheque to which, owing to fraud or forgery, the customer has no title and may therefore find itself liable to the true owner of the cheque. Fortunately, in terms of Section 4 of the *Cheques Act 1957*, the bank has statutory protection in such circumstances provided it acts in good faith and without negligence and acts for a customer. Where a banker, in good faith and without negligence, credits a customer's account with the amount of a cheque and then receives payment for the cheque and the customer has no title, or a defective title, the banker does not incur any liability to the true owner of the cheque.

You will remember from the first chapter that it was not particularly easy to define who was and who wasn't a customer, yet in order to benefit from the protection in Section 4 of the *1957 Act*, the banker must act for a customer. There is no definition in either the *Bills of Exchange Act* or the *Cheques Act 1957* as to whom is to be regarded as a customer. Obviously if someone maintains an account with the bank, then that person is a customer.

It is important to determine, however, at which point the person actually becomes a customer. Does someone who asks the bank to collect a cheque and credit the proceeds to a new account with the bank immediately become a customer or must there be a course of dealing between the bank and the customer before he/she can truly be regarded as a customer?

The common view is that, as the law stands at present, a customer is a person for whom a bank has opened an account, and the relationship of banker and customer begins when the first cheque is paid in and accepted by the bank for collection and not merely when that cheque is paid.

There is nothing in the Acts to tell us what is meant by in good faith and without negligence; however, through time there have been several court cases, the outcome of which have given indications on what is expected of a bank acting "without negligence". The courts have taken a stringent view of the banker's duty to act without negligence when collecting cheques, as the following examples illustrate.

Case study

If a bank fails to obtain satisfactory references for a new customer, the failure to do so may be regarded as negligent.

Ladbroke -v- Todd, 1914

A crossed cheque was stolen from a pillar box by a third party, who forged the payee's indorsement, impersonated him and opened an account with the bank to which the cheque was credited. The bank made no enquiries as to the new customer's character and was held to have acted for a customer but to have acted negligently.

A bank will be guilty of negligence if it collects for a customer who is a director of a limited company, a cheque made payable to the company and indorsed by the director, on behalf of the company to his own order.

A L Underwood Limited -v- Bank of Liverpool and Martins Limited, 1924

The sole director of a company came into possession of cheques payable to the company. The director was called A L Underwood and the cheques were payable to A L Underwood Limited and Underwood held all of the shares in the company but one. Underwood indorsed the cheques on behalf of the company and paid them into his own account. The bank made no enquiries and accepted the cheques for credit of the account.

A third party who had been granted a charge over the company's assets raised an action against the bank and it was held in the case that the actions of the director were so unusual as to put the bank on enquiry and the failure of the bank to make suitable enquiries amounted to negligence on the bank's part.

Similarly a bank should not credit the account of a partner of a firm with cheques payable to the firm unless it makes enquiries and is completely satisfied that the transaction is in order.

Where operations of an unusual or abnormal character occur on an account, the banker must be vigilant. If the operations on the account are incompatible with the known circumstances of the customer, it should put the bank on enquiry.

Guardians of St John, Hampstead -v- Barclays Bank Limited

The opening of an account with a small cheque one day followed by the paying in of a large cheque the next day was one of the incidents which led the Court to find the bank guilty of negligence.

Accepting a cheque crossed "Account Payee" for someone other than the named payee has for some time been regarded as acting negligently. The position has been put beyond doubt by the *Cheques Act 1992* which prohibits such practice in all but a very small number of circumstances.

System for clearing cheques

When a cheque is issued it can take some time to reach the bank account on which it was drawn. We shall now take a look at how a cheque finds its way from the customer's cheque book to their bank account.

The method of clearing cheques may vary from bank to bank but the basic principles remain the same. When a cheque is issued, the payee of the cheque will take it and any other cheques payable to them (and any cash) to their bank and have their account credited with the total sum. The cash paid in does not need to clear or be confirmed by anyone.

The cheques paid in fall into two categories:

- those that have been drawn on the same branch of the bank as the one where the payee is making the lodgement – sometimes called house cheques

- those that have been drawn on other branches and other banks.

The cheques that have been drawn on the branch of the bank where the payee is paying in should not be too difficult to deal with – the banker will look at the cheques and decide whether they will be paid or dishonoured; if they are to be paid they will be debited to the drawers' accounts. If any cheque is to be dishonoured, it will be returned to the person making the lodgement. As soon as a house cheque has been paid, the payee can have full credit for its proceeds.

The cheques that have been drawn on other banks and branches are not quite as straightforward. These cheques must find their way to the account-holding banks and branches in order that the relative bankers can make a decision on whether or not the cheques are to be paid.

We shall look at how this is done shortly, but you can see that there is a potential problem for both the payee and the payee's banker:

- the payee has provided goods or services but even when the cheques received from customers are lodged to their account, it is still not certain that they have been paid

- the banker has permitted funds to be credited to the account in the name of the payee, but has no guarantee that he will not have to debit the account at a later date should the cheques not be honoured when they are presented to the relative account-holding bankers.

The proceeds of cheques that have not yet been paid by the drawee bank are known as uncleared funds or uncleared effects. Banks will accept uncleared funds for lodgement into an account and the amount will immediately be added to the balance of the customer's account. If a bank statement were produced for the customer the following day, or were the customer to check their statement online, the full amount of the lodgement would be shown as being credited to the customer's account, but the customer would not be entitled to draw against these uncleared funds until they had been cleared. The banker accepting the lodgement would defer full credit for the amount of uncleared cheques for a number of days.

If cheques were presented prior to the funds being cleared, the banker would be entitled to return the cheques unpaid. If the banker permitted the cheques to be paid then, while technically the account of the customer would remain in credit, if the banker looks at cleared funds only, an overdraft has emerged and the customer will be charged interest – sometimes called deferment interest.

The cheques that still have to be cleared will be remitted to a processing area within the bank. These cheques fall into two categories:

•   those that have been drawn on branches of the bank

•   those that have been drawn on other banks.

Cheques that have been drawn on other branches of the same bank will be processed within that bank. Cheques that have been drawn on other banks will be passed to the banks concerned. The collecting bank will receive payment from the drawee bank, but it is likely that the drawee bank will hold other cheques that are drawn on the collecting bank. The two banks will therefore exchange the cheques and make settlement only for the net sum due. Depending on the value of these cheques, one bank will owe payment to another. Once received, the collecting bank will either pass the cheques to the branches upon which these cheques are drawn, or as is now more likely, will remit these to a centralised location within the bank.

As a result of consumer pressure regarding the length of time taken for cheques to clear in the UK, procedural changes were made to standardise the treatment of cheques by members of the Cheque and Credit Clearing Company and the Belfast Bankers Clearing Committee.

The information regarding when a deposited cheque will start to earn interest, when funds may be withdrawn against a deposited cheque and when a cheque may be reclaimed from a beneficiary's account is expressed in terms of, for example, "T + 2 (days)". The precise definition of T will need to be made clear in the terms and conditions of each account, taking account of branch cut-off times, and it may also vary according to the way in which the cheque is lodged, for example at an automated deposit facility, at a post office or by post. Normally, for a counter deposit, T will be the day of deposit if it is made before the advertised cut-off time at the bank counter. If the deposit is made after this cut-off time, then T would be the following business day. For a postal deposit, T would be deemed to be the day that the cheque is received by the bank.

Assuming that a cheque has been deposited in an interest bearing account, it will start either to earn interest or reduce the amount of overdraft interest charged by no later than T + 2.

In this case, interest should start to accrue no later than Wednesday.

When a cheque is deposited to a current or basic bank account, it will be available for withdrawal no later than the start of business on T + 4.

In this case, the funds should be available for withdrawal no later than start of business on Friday.

For a savings account from which withdrawals are allowed, funds will be available no later than start of business on T + 6.

In this scenario, the funds will be available for withdrawal no later than start of business on the Tuesday of the following week.

Regarding the fate of cheques, no cheque will be reclaimed from a beneficiary customer's account any later than T + 6 without the agreement of the beneficiary customer, or unless the beneficiary was a knowing party to a fraud. This proposition applies to all types of account. The practical implication of this is that if a cheque is deposited on a Monday, it will be deemed to be irrevocably paid if it has not been dishonoured or reversed by the close of business on the Tuesday of the following week.

Question   **5**

Go to question section starting on page 243

Check with the answer at the back of the book.

Review

Now consider the main learning points which were introduced in this chapter.

Go through them and tick each one when you are happy that you fully understand each point.

Then check back to the objectives at the beginning of the chapter and match them to the learning points.

Reread any section you are unsure of before moving on.

A cheque is an unconditional order in writing drawn by one party on another, who must be a banker, signed by the drawer, requiring the banker to pay on demand a sum certain in money to or to the order of a specified person or to bearer.

☐

Any alteration to a cheque must be made with the consent of the drawer who should either sign or initial at each point on the cheque where an alteration has been made.

☐

A crossing is a direction to the bank placed on the face of the cheque by the drawer that the amount should be paid only to a banker or through a bank account.

☐

When a cheque is truncated it is retained at some point in the clearing process.

☐

If a bank is to return a cheque unpaid, great care must be taken to ensure that there are no funds of the customer available for payment of the cheque that has been presented.

☐

A bank is legally prohibited from making payment of a cheque if the customer has countermanded payment, if the customer has died, if the customer has been declared bankrupt, if the customer is insane or if the banker has knowledge of any defect in title of the person presenting the cheque for payment.

☐

Where the customer's signature has been forged on a cheque, the banker cannot debit the account if the cheque is paid.

☐

If a cheque lodged has been drawn on other banks and branches they must find their way to the account-holding banks and branches in order that the relative bankers can make a decision on whether or not the cheques are to be paid.

☐

There are standardised timescales for clearing cheques. These timescales are determined by the way and times when items were lodged to accounts, along with the type of account involved.

☐

Key words in this chapter are given below. There is space to write your own revision notes and to add any other words or phrases that you want to remember.

bill of exchange

drawer

payee

post dated

stale cheques

negotiable instrument

attachment of funds

crossings

truncation

countermand of payment

house cheque

uncleared funds/uncleared effects

deferment

deferment interest

Multiple choice questions   **5**

Try these self-test questions to assess your understanding of what you have read in this chapter.

The answers are at the back of the book.

1 The person who writes a cheque payable to another party is referred to as which one of the following?

A   the payee

B   the drawee

C   the drawer

D   the creditor

2 Which one of the following is not a requirement for a cheque to be valid?

A   it must be in writing

B   it must be conditional

C   it must be for a sum certain in money

D   it must be paid to the order of a specified person

3 If a cheque requires to be altered, which one of the following courses of action would apply?

A   A fresh cheque must be issued

B   Alterations must be signed or initialled by the drawer

C   Alterations must be signed or initialled by the payee

D   The drawer must contact the bank to authorise payment

Multiple choice questions   **5**

4 What is the consequence of a bank dishonouring a cheque where funds are actually available?

A   the bank may be prosecuted

B   the bank may be liable to pay compensation

C   the bank may be liable to pay damages

D   there is no consequence to the bank

5 Your customer has a basic bank account and they lodge a cheque drawn on another bank for £250 to their account on Thursday. When will these funds clear?

A   Immediately

B   The following Monday

C   The following Wednesday

D   The following Thursday

6 Which one of the following is a description of house cheques?

A   cheques drawn on the head office of the bank

B   cheques drawn on the same branch as that of the payee

C   temporary cheques issued at the counter pending issue of a new cheque book

D   cheques drawn on any clearing bank

Multiple choice questions   **5**

7   The latest period it would take for a cheque to clear is:

A   4 business days

B   7 business days

C   5 business days

D   6 business days

8   James is a company director. On 2 September he writes and signs a cheque on behalf of his company. On 3 September he dies. Which one of the following would be the consequence of James's death in respect of the payment?

A   the cheque must be returned unpaid

B   the cheque may be paid but must be countersigned by another director

C   the cheque may be processed in the normal manner

D   a duplicate cheque must be issued

6   Plastic and Electronic Banking

Objectives

By the end of this chapter, you should be able to:

- Outline the functions of online and telephone banking.

- Describe what is meant by electronic transfer of funds at the point of sale and how this process works.

- Explain electronic funds transfer.

- Describe the use of plastic cards in banking.

Introduction

If you have been working in banking for any length of time, you will be aware that the ways in which customers carry out their financial affairs and communicate with their bank has altered significantly. We are now going to consider how technology has enabled the range of bank services and money transmission methods to be extended, particularly online and telephone banking, and how funds can be transferred electronically. We will also look at the increasing use of plastic cards, especially credit and debit cards, in banking and money transmission.

Telephone and online banking

Most banks now offer customers some form of direct banking facility – indeed, some of the newer players in the market operate solely as direct banks. With direct banking, the customer has access to their account 24 hours a day, 7 days a week, by telephone or internet, identifying themselves by a security password.

The main advantages of offering direct banking are that:

- routine enquires can be dealt with directly, thus removing the need for branch staff to deal with these enquiries and allowing them to concentrate on those tasks that can only be dealt with in the branch

- the organisation can provide a better service to customers through the use of specialist staff and software

- new players can enter the market at a much lower cost; in the past, the financing costs of setting up a bank with a branch network were significant; direct banking with the provision of telephone and internet banking represents an entry route to the market at a much lower cost.

Telephone banking

Some organisations operate solely as telephone banks, whilst other financial services organisations offer telephone banking as part of a wider range of options available to their customers. When using a telephone banking service the customer will usually have the option of using either an Automated Telephone Service or of speaking to an adviser.

If a customer uses an automated telephone service, when they telephone the organisation they are greeted by a recorded message that will offer them some service options, such as "press 1 for balance enquiries, press 2 for recent transactions" etc. The call will then be dealt with automatically, for example, under option 1, the system will advise the customer of the relevant balance without the need for an adviser to intervene. This is called Interactive Voice Response, which we will consider in more detail shortly. Alternatively, the customer may prefer to speak to an adviser, perhaps because the subject of their call is more complex.

Before looking at some of the services that a customer can access through telephone banking, we'll consider some of the systems which underpin telephone banking.

Automatic Call Distribution

Calls coming into a call centre do not appear in an orderly fashion but arrive randomly. There is a telephone system that handles incoming calls in a consistent and controlled manner – Automatic Call Distribution, abbreviated to ACD. The ACD acts as a gatekeeper to the call centre which means that all the incoming calls are directed to it before they are distributed to the advisers. If a customer phones the call centre, they will go first through their telecommunications provider who in turn will send the call on to the call centre. The ACD will accept the call and consult with a set of rules that have been programmed into it, to decide where in the centre the call should go.

Some of the features of an ACD include the ability to:

- place incoming calls in a queuing system and make sure that they are answered in the correct order

- manage the queue of calls

- direct calls to the right staff

- allow messaging systems to take details from customers if no advisers are available to take the call within a specified period of time

- allow Integrated Voice Response (IVR).

Following on from the final point, most if not all financial services call centres offer an IVR service. This means that the customer can request information or even carry out a transaction without having to speak to an adviser. When the call arrives at the centre, the customer has the option of either talking to an adviser or using the IVR service. The customer communicates their choice by using the keypad on their phone. If the customer chooses to use the IVR service, their call is forwarded to the computer system. At this point the customer hears an automated, recorded voice which asks the customer what service(s) they wish to use. In response to these questions, the customer presses keys on their telephone which transmit a signal to the computer. Alternatively, the system may have voice recognition software that would allow the customer to give instructions verbally and the system can recognise this and take the appropriate action. For example, this system could be used to request a re-advice of PIN and, assuming that the system's security thresholds are reached, the customer will receive this re-advice by text message. This is a much quicker response than were the PIN to be posted to the customer.

However, not all the services on offer are available through IVR. Some of the more sensitive requests are available solely by the customer talking to an adviser. An additional factor affecting the availability of IVR for particular transactions is the level of security required by the organisation. The sophistication of the system will affect how security requirements can be met and thus determines the levels of services that can be provided by IVR.

When using telephone banking, a customer can access the following services:

- obtaining a balance enquiry

- identifying recent transactions

- transferring funds between accounts

- paying a bill

- standing orders

- amending/cancelling a direct debit

- share dealing

- arranging an overdraft

- third party payments.

- Re-advice of PIN

We have already looked at some of these services earlier in the course, so we'll examine some of the others in more detail now.

Obtaining a balance enquiry/Identifying recent transactions

To access this service, the customer first has to prove to the bank that they are indeed the customer they say they are by using a security code or answering some questions to verify their identity. They will then be able to access the information requested either from an adviser or through IVR.

Transferring funds

As you already know, if a customer wishes to transfer the same amount of funds between two of their accounts on the same date each month, they should set up a monthly standing order. However, if the amount and date of transfer is variable, they have the option of giving this instruction to the call centre which can then make the transfer for them. There is usually also the option of having the transfer carried out immediately or diarised for some future date.

Paying a bill

Most call centres provide customers with a facility whereby they can instruct bills to be paid over the phone. All that the customer needs to do is give the centre information about the bill payment and the adviser processes the transaction through the account.

Share dealing

The call centre also allows banks to offer the service of receiving telephone instructions from customers to buy and sell stocks and shares. In the past, only written instructions were accepted from customers who wished to buy or sell on the stock market, but now, provided that the customer has completed the appropriate level of security, the call will normally be passed through to a stockbroker who will attend to the purchase or sale on behalf of the customer.

Third party payments

A third party payment is a payment made by a customer through their financial services provider to another person. It has been possible to make this type of payment for many years by using a bank giro credit at a bank branch. Normally the funds are debited from the customer's account on the date requested and sent through the clearing system to reach the beneficiary's account in two to three working days. It is possible to effect these payments through the telephone centre, by supplying the relevant information and the payment date.

Re-advice of PIN

If a customer has forgotten the PIN for their plastic card, or if this number has been disclosed to another party, they can contact the telephone centre to either receive a new PIN or to be re-advised of their existing PIN. As explained earlier, this can be done either through the post, or by text message.

Online banking

All banks now have their own websites which allow customers to obtain information on the products and services offered.

There are two types of internet banks:

- stand alone internet banks offering competitive interest rates and service charges due to having lower overheads than their high street competitors

- traditional banks providing branch, telephone and internet banking facilities.

The advantages of internet banking are that:

- services are available 24 hours a day, 7 days a week

- the time and effort involved in visiting branches are removed, as customers can transact their business if they have access to the appropriate technology – personal computer, laptop or mobile application.

- fees are often lower than traditional banking fees

- despite concerns about security, the technology used ensures the privacy and safety of the customers' financial information

- customers can check the balances of their accounts, transfer funds between accounts and make electronic bill payments.

An internet banking service normally provides customers with the following services:

- current balances and recent transactions

- copy statements

- information on automated payments

- the ability to cancel and/or amend standing orders and direct debits

- application for various money transmission, savings and lending products.

In addition, there will normally be information about the organisation, such as a history and current structure, information on current corporate social responsibility programmes, environmental initiatives being undertaken, contact information, etc.

Electronic Funds Transfer at Point Of Sale (EFTPOS)

When the use of cheques and credit cards increased, it was thought that we were heading for the cashless society, but increased use of technology in money transmission means that we could be heading towards the chequeless society. This can be evidenced with the number of large retailers, such as petrol stations and supermarkets, who will no longer accept cheques as a means of payment. EFTPOS stands for Electronic Transfer of Funds at Point Of Sale and involves the transfer of funds from the account of a customer directly into the bank account of the retailer at the time a sale is made. There is no need for the customer to write a cheque and the retailer will not have to wait for the funds to clear.

The procedure for making payment is very safe and convenient. The customer has a debit or credit card which bears their signature. This card can be used to make payments and withdraw cash either at an ATM or in a bank branch. When making a payment, the retailer will either swipe the card or insert it into a reader and the customer authorises the transaction by inserting their PIN into a keypad. The reader will then communicate with the bank's technology to authorise and process the payment.

The major banks are either members of Switch or Visa which operate EFTPOS systems in the UK. These systems are paperless in so far as debiting the customer's account and transferring funds to the retailer's account are concerned.

Electronic funds transfer – CHAPS

CHAPS stands for Clearing House Automated Payment System. The organisation's members comprise the leading UK banks, along with the Bank of England and some international banks with a significant presence in the UK.

CHAPS is an electronic credit transfer system for sending same day value sterling payments from one member bank (a settlement bank) to another. The payments are same day value as it is not necessary to wait for funds credited to an account to clear. Every CHAPS payment is unconditional, guaranteed and cannot be recalled once sent.

CHAPS commenced in 1984. The system opens at 6.00hrs daily, although member banks need not be open at that time. The latest time that a payment may be made is 16.00hrs. The system is used for high-value transactions where it would not be appropriate to use the traditional clearing system. For example, larger house purchase transactions and the settlement of high-value transactions between organisations. We will now discuss the Faster Payments system which is now used for lower value transactions where the parties involved do not wish to use the clearing system.

Given the number and value of payments handled by CHAPS, the system has a very high level of built-in security measures to prevent unauthorised or fraudulent transfers being initiated. In 2007 almost £70 trillion was processed through the CHAPS system.

Faster Payments

Banks now offer customers the Faster Payments service. Under this service, it is possible to make automated payments that are guaranteed to reach the beneficiaries account within two hours – although in reality receipt is almost instantaneous. Whilst banks have offered same-day payments services in the past (through CHAPS), these have been targeted at high-value transactions. Faster Payments on the other hand is targeted at smaller value transactions of up to £100,000.

Credit cards

Credit cards have been in use in this country since the early 1970s although their use and the spread of ownership increased during the 1980s and they are now a very widely used method of making payments and for obtaining credit facilities. A credit card is a plastic card which can be used by the cardholder to purchase goods and services which are paid for at a later date.

There are currently two dominant groups who operate international networks – Visa and MasterCard. All the main banks, building societies and other organisations offer their own versions of either or both of these cards. You should familiarise yourself with the type(s) of card(s) that are offered by your own organisation.

The essential features of a credit card are:

- the purchase of goods and services on credit subject to an agreed overall limit

- the issue of regular statements by the credit card company

- the option for the customer of either paying all of the sums due to the credit card company or electing to pay off only a portion of the sums due (minimum amount or 3 - 5% whichever is the greater) and paying interest on the remainder.

Application procedure

A credit card account operates independently of a customer's other accounts with the bank, and the relationship between the bank and the cardholder differs from the traditional banker/customer relationship.

It is not necessary for a person to maintain an account with the bank before they can be issued with a credit card. It is initiated by a separate agreement between the bank and its customer regulating the issue of the credit card and the debtor/creditor relationship that exists between the parties. In addition, due to the element of credit involved, the bank will have to be satisfied that the customer can be considered creditworthy for the amount of their limit. The customer completes an application form as the basis of the agreement between them and the bank. The application form also provides the bank with a great deal of information about the customer, such as employer, salary, house owner or tenant, marital status, number of children, etc.

The creditworthiness of the applicant is assessed by credit scoring.

Use of the credit card

Provided that the issuer is satisfied with the creditworthiness of the customer, a card and PIN will be issued and the customer will be granted a credit limit. The customer can then use the card to make purchases up to the amount of the limit on the account. The card is used to pay for goods and services in the same way as described earlier – the retailer either swipes the card or inserts it into a reader, after which the customer authorises the transaction with their PIN and the transaction is processed.

A credit card can also be used for postal, internet and telephone transactions; the card number being quoted over the phone, input to a screen or noted on an order form sent in the post. Cash can be withdrawn via ATMs using the credit card by the cardholder inputing a PIN notified to them at the time the card was issued. This withdrawal will be treated by the credit card company as a cash advance and so interest will accrue from the date of the transaction.

Joint credit cards are not offered, but the customer has the option of applying for other persons to be issued with cards on the account. For example, a husband and wife may both have credit cards and the same account will be debited regardless of whose card is used, but only one person will be liable for repayment of the debt.

Customers have the option if having statements posted to them, or viewing them online. The information on the statement includes:

- their limit

- the transactions that have been made with the card(s)

- any payments that have been received

- any interest that has been debited to the account

- the current balance

- the amount of available credit remaining

- an estimate of the interest which will appear on the next statement based on the current balance.

The cardholder is not required to make any payment to the issuer of the credit card until 21 days after the date of the statement. The latest date for receipt of a payment is shown on the statement. Depending on when a purchase is made, credit cards can provide a period of up to 56 days of interest-free credit.

On receipt of a statement a cardholder has the option of:

- repaying the whole balance by the due date shown on the statement, or

- repaying a minimum amount or 3 - 5% (whichever is the greater) of the balance by the due date (provided that the balance is more than £5, otherwise the whole amount due must be repaid).

Should the cardholder elect not to clear the balance due, interest will be charged monthly from the statement date on any outstanding balance not repaid.

Company credit cards

Companies can make use of credit card facilities to help them control business expenses and manage cash flow and at the same time provide their staff who incur regular expenses with a simple and convenient payment method in the UK or abroad. An overall limit is agreed between the company and the bank. Thereafter, designated members of company staff are given a credit card with set limits within the company's overall agreed limit. Each card issued normally bears the name of the company and of the cardholder. Statements are usually produced in respect of each cardholder with an additional summary statement showing the total amount due for payment from all cardholders. Settlement of the sum due is normally effected by direct debit from the company's bank account.

Charge cards

Charge cards are similar to credit cards in that a customer is allocated a limit and receives a monthly statement, but the important difference is that the statement balances require to be settled in full each month. For customers in higher income brackets, banks offer "Gold Cards" or "Premier Cards" – both of these would tend to have limits that are higher than usual. Automatic overdraft facilities are also included.

Store credit/charge cards

Many department stores and other retailers have introduced their own cards which operate in direct competition to credit cards issued by banks. The main advantage for retailers, apart from the interest they receive, is that the ready availability of credit should lead to increased sales. Retailers will also hope that customers will buy goods from their store using the store card.

Stores which offer their own store cards also accept other credit cards issued under the auspices of MasterCard or Visa. Store cards operate in the same way as credit cards in that a monthly statement is provided and the customers have the option of paying off all that is outstanding or paying only a portion of the outstanding debt and paying interest on the remainder.

Question   **6**

Go to question section starting on page 243

Check with the answer at the back of the book.

Review

Now consider the main learning points which were introduced in this chapter.

Go through them and tick each one when you are happy that you fully understand each point.

Then check back to the objectives at the beginning of the chapter and match them to the learning points.

Reread any section you are unsure of before moving on.

With direct banking, the customer has access to their account 24 hours a day, 7 days a week, either by telephone or internet.

☐

Automatic Call Distribution acts as a gatekeeper to a call centre.

☐

When using telephone banking, a customer can obtain a balance enquiry, identify recent transactions, transfer funds between accounts, pay a bill, obtain information on standing orders, amend/cancel a direct debit, give share dealing instructions, arrange an overdraft, make third party payments, or request a re-advice of PIN.

☐

An internet banking service normally provides customers with the following services: current balances and recent transactions, copy statements, information on automated payments, cancel/amend standing orders and direct debits, apply for certain products.

☐

EFTPOS facilitates the transfer of funds from the account of a customer directly into the bank account of the retailer at the time a sale is made.

☐

CHAPS is an electronic credit transfer system for sending same day value sterling payments from one member bank to another.

☐

A credit card can be used by the cardholder to purchase goods and services which are paid for at a later date.

☐

 Key words in this chapter are given below. There is space to write your own revision notes and to add any other words or phrases that you want to remember.

direct banking

telephone banking

Automated Telephone Service

Automatic Call Distribution

Interactive Voice Response

EFTPOS

CHAPS

settlement bank

same day value

CHAPS

Faster Payments

Multiple choice questions   **6**

Try these self-test questions to assess your understanding of what you have read in this chapter.
The answers are at the back of the book.

1   Which one of the following money transmission media is most suitable for same day, large value transactions?

A   cheques and credit clearing

B   bank giro credit

C   BACS

D   CHAPS

2   The upper limit for a payment to be processed through the Faster Payments system is:

A   £50,000

B   £100,000

C   £250,000

D   £500,000

3   Which one of the following will not normally be included on a credit card statement?

A   credit limit

B   card expiry date

C   interest debited this month

D   applicable interest rate

Multiple choice questions   **6**

4   William has a Visa credit card. What are the maximum days of interest-free credit normally available to him when using the card?

A   14 days

B   28 days

C   30 days

D   56 days

7 Lending

Objectives

By the end of this chapter, you should be able to:

- Present a structured approach to the credit assessment process.

- Describe the main lending products offered by banks.

- Explain the nature and purpose of credit scoring.

Introduction

In this chapter we will look at the general principles of good lending practice, in particular the canons or principles of lending. Lending money is an important part of a banking business but it must be done properly and prudently, otherwise the bank may sustain loss. Much of bank lending is now credit scored, so we'll also look at this area.

What is lending?

As you know, banks accept money on deposit from customers and pay them interest on the sums deposited. Naturally the bank must find the money to pay the depositor's interest and must also make a profit for the benefit of the bank's shareholders. One of the ways the bank achieves this is to lend or advance the money deposited to its customers. The bank will be paid interest on the amount advanced and the rate of interest charged by the bank will be greater than the rate of interest paid by the bank on deposits. The difference between the two rates, the margin, is part of the bank's profit.

In addition, a bank normally charges customers an arrangement fee for advances. An arrangement fee is a charge made to customers to cover the cost to the bank of arranging the loan. It takes account of the cost of staff time in setting up the facility, the costs involved in setting up the account on the bank's computer system, the costs of preparing supporting documentation, etc. Normally an arrangement fee is lower when an existing facility is being renewed as opposed to the setting up of a completely new advance. This is because it is less time consuming to review an existing facility than it is to set up a completely new facility.

The amount of the arrangement fee will be negotiated between the bank and the customer at the time the borrowing is agreed. While there will be some discussion between the bank and the customer as to the level of the arrangement fee, there are some parameters around which the banker will wish to operate. You should identify what these parameters are in your own organisation.

If a bank lends money to an individual, firm or company and the borrower is unable to repay the advance, not only will the bank lose the interest it requires to pay depositors, it will also lose some of the capital sum deposited and will have to repay these deposits and interest out of profits. You will therefore appreciate that, while lending is an important and profitable business tool of a bank, it is vitally important that bankers acquire, develop and use lending skills to ensure that all lending remains safe and profitable.

The principles of lending

Lending money is not an exact science; that is, it is not possible to work out some formula or apply a certain theory and by doing so guarantee that the amount advanced to a customer will be repaid with interest. However, there are general principles of good lending or canons of lending, which, if applied consistently, should reduce the guesswork and hence risk involved in lending to a customer.

In this course, we are going to review the factors a banker should consider when assessing a credit proposition. The general principles of good lending can be broken down into five categories:

- the borrower
- the lending proposition
- security
- repayment
- remuneration.

The borrower

A bank's agreement to lend should depend on its view of the customer's current and future ability to repay. It is therefore essential that the bank obtains as much information as possible regarding the financial affairs of the potential borrower and is confident that it can rely fully on the information provided.

The bank should be considering how well it knows its customer. The bank's records should disclose how long the customer – if in fact they are at this stage a customer – has maintained a relationship or connection with the bank and what their previous track record has been; for example, have their accounts been maintained in a satisfactory manner in the past? Any unauthorised or excess borrowing? Have previous loans been repaid in accordance with the agreed repayment programme?

If the proposed borrower is an existing customer, the bank should already know quite a lot about them. If the customer's salary is mandated to the bank, there will be a fairly complete picture of the customer's income and expenditure. For example, if the customer is paid monthly and in the last week of every month the account is becoming more and more overdrawn, how does the customer expect to make the repayment instalments on the loan they have requested?

When looking at a request from an existing customer for a loan or overdraft for personal purposes, the banker more often than not will have all the information required to make the decision unless the request has come about as a result of a fundamental change in the customer's circumstances. A request for additional borrowing as a result of a major career change would be an example of this. Credit scoring is used in many cases and we'll look at this in the next section. The same cannot be said for requests from non-customers or requests for advances for business purposes.

Other factors the bank should consider, especially in respect of advances for business purposes, include:

- the age or, more importantly, the maturity of the borrower

- qualifications and experience

- financial acumen

- integrity and reliability

- organisational ability and efficiency.

In order to comply with the law, banks do not normally lend to individuals under the age of eighteen. It is more important, however, to consider the maturity of the borrower; for example, have they thought out their business proposition and do they appear to have the ability to see their proposition to conclusion?

Many people in business have no formal qualifications, but unless such qualifications are essential to the successful operation of the business, for example an accountancy practice, experience is more important. The banker must consider whether or not the borrower has the qualifications and/or the experience to enable them to undertake the business successfully.

Another important skill is in the demonstration of financial acumen and the ability to keep proper records and accounts. If the customer has an overdraft limit, can they operate within that limit? Does the customer know how many items they must sell before a profit is earned (that is, at what level will the business start to break even?) If they sell goods at a certain price, do they know how much it has cost to produce the items and does this price also cover overheads and result in a profit?

Unless the customer is well known to you, you should seek references from reliable sources, such as from the customer's previous bankers. You should also be confident that the customer has the ability to carry out their business as they could soon get into trouble if deadlines are missed or goods fail to be delivered to customers on time. The banker should be satisfied that the customer is aware of their capabilities and do not, for example, overstretch their resources.

The customer's business

It is also important that the banker gets to know something of the customer's business activities and their overall business strategy:

- Is the customer involved in a highly competitive business where competitors are always trying to undercut each other?

- If your customer gets involved in this, how will a price reduction affect the figures provided to you at the time the application for the advance was made?

- How will it affect the customer's ability to repay the loan?

- Is the customer's business subject to seasonal fluctuations? For example, a small hotel in a seaside town, a producer of Christmas trees.

It may be necessary to ask your customer lots of pertinent questions before you can fully consider a lending proposition.

The lending proposition

The crucial questions to consider when analysing the lending proposition are:

- What is the purpose of the advance?

- How much of an advance is required?

- When will the advance be repaid?

The banker should also consider whether the facilities requested are within the bank's Credit Policy. For example, a bank may have a limit on how much it will lend to a particular sector; there may be government or Bank of England directives on lending to a particular sector. In addition, the type of facility and the purpose may not be a recognised "product" of the bank and it may be more appropriate to refer the customer to a subsidiary or associate company of the bank involved in, say, leasing or factoring.

■ What is the purpose of the advance?

The purpose of the advance should be clearly defined and understood by both the customer and the banker. Is the lending proposition basically sound? Has it been thought through fully by the customer and do they have any projections or figures, such as a cash flow forecast, to support their request?

The banker must also be satisfied that the advance is for a legal and proper purpose. In most cases this will not pose a problem.

As well as ensuring that the transaction is legal and within the powers of the borrower, it is just as important to be satisfied that the purpose of the loan has been well thought out by the customer and that they will be in a position to repay the loan in line with the agreed repayment programme.

■ How much of an advance is required?

Obviously it is essential for the bank (and the customer) to know how much of a loan is required and/or how much the overdraft limit should be. One point to remember here is that there is as much risk of a loan not being repaid because the borrower has requested not enough of an advance as there is when a customer borrows too much money.

Sometimes a customer may request the maximum amount they think that a bank may lend to them, even if this amount is less than they actually need to finance the intended purpose, and you should bear in mind that if the project is not a success, the customer may not be able to repay the advance.

Example

Your customer wants to expand his business and requests a loan of £45,000 to purchase additional equipment costing £50,000. What you and the customer must bear in mind is that the extra equipment may involve an increase in other costs, such as the amount of electrical power used, additional wages or overtime costs or the purchase of additional raw materials. However, there could be a timing difference here as your customer may need to pay the supplier for the raw materials before receiving payment from his customers.

If your customer has not borrowed enough and cannot finance the extra costs, a situation could evolve where he has a piece of equipment he cannot afford to use and, more importantly from the bank's point of view, a piece of equipment which is not earning its keep! The additional income anticipated from the expansion will not now materialise and your customer may be unable to repay the loan.

To ensure that the correct level of advance has been requested, the customer's request should be supported by a cash flow projection which can be a statement showing how much "cash" the customer presently has, what their projected income and expenditure will be and therefore how much cash they will have at the end of the period. The cash flow forecast should of course include the customer's own drawings from the business and the capital and interest payments due to the bank.

It is important that this cash flow projection reflects when cash is received into the business and paid out of the business. "Cash" can encompass physical cash, cheques, automated payments, etc. When preparing a cash flow projection, the customer may estimate, for example, that sales in January will be £5,000. However, if the business allows 60 days credit, this £5,000 should not appear in the cash flow forecast until March as that is the month in which payment will be received and lodged to the account. Similarly, payments made should be included in the cash flow, not when the debt is incurred, but when the business will make the payment. In this case, if the business buys materials for £2,500 in May, but is allowed 30 days credit, this amount should appear in the cash flow projection for June.

When considering the amount of the loan requested, the bank should also estimate the value of the business, in particular how much the customer has invested personally. It is worthwhile remembering that if the customer has invested £10,000 in their business and they are requesting to lend £15,000, they are asking the bank to invest more money in the business than they have – in other words for the bank to take a greater risk than they are prepared to take. This is considered as the customer's level of commitment.

■ **When will the advance be repaid?**

Overdrafts are repayable on demand but term loans can be for periods in excess of 20 years depending on the type of proposal. The banker may wish to consider, for example, whether the loan will be repaid within the effective lifetime of the piece of equipment to be purchased. This also applies to personal lending. For example, some banks are willing to provide car loans repayable over up to five years in respect of a new car but not for a loan to purchase a car which is seven years old as this would mean that when the car is ten years old and possibly no longer roadworthy, the customer will still have a further two years of the loan to repay.

Security

Any decision by a bank to lend money to one of its customers will depend on its view of the customer's present and future ability to repay the advance from their own resources. In other words, any proposition should be able to stand on its own without the need for security. The bank, however, may wish to safeguard against unforeseen circumstances or risk and for the customer's obligations to the bank to be supported by acceptable security. (We will look at security in detail in the next chapter.) What the banker should be considering is what value can realistically be placed on any security provided, how easy will it be to convert the security to cash should the need arise and how easy it will be to actually take the security.

Repayment

It is important for the bank to know when a loan will be repaid and that the customer is in fact able to repay the loan within the agreed repayment period. Again, asking the customer to prepare a cash flow forecast will help both the bank and the customer to agree a sensible repayment programme. There is obviously no point in the bank stipulating a repayment programme of £250 per month if it is clear that the most that the customer can afford to repay is £125 per month.

The bank will obviously not wish the loan to be outstanding for any longer than it considers necessary or prudent, but the fact is that the longer the term of the loan, the smaller the amount of the repayment instalments. It is also fair to say that the longer a loan is outstanding, the greater the risk of something happening that will increase the risk of the loan not being repaid.

So far we have looked mainly at advances for business purposes. In many respects it is easier to consider repayment of a loan for personal purposes, especially if the customer has a regular salary, even better if paid straight into their bank account. It will be easy to determine the amount of the customer's income and further investigation will reveal the customer's regular outgoings – again examination of the bank account will be useful as this will show regular standing orders, direct debits, mortgage payments, etc. From all this information the bank will be able to see the amount that the customer is comfortably able to repay on a monthly basis.

Remuneration

Remuneration is very important as this is one of the ways in which the bank makes a profit! At the beginning of this chapter we discussed how the bank accepts money from one set of customers at a certain rate of interest and lends to another set of customers at a higher rate of interest. If the bank is to remain in business, it is essential that the margin between the rates is sufficient to ensure that the bank makes a profit in lending to the customer. We have already discussed arrangement fees which are put in place by banks to cover the costs of setting up a loan facility, and these fees also contribute to the overall remuneration received by a bank.

A final point to consider is that the risk being taken by a bank in granting a loan should be reflected in the reward it receives. It would therefore be reasonable for a bank to charge a higher rate of interest than usual if it considers that it is taking a higher risk in making the loan available. Similarly, it would not be unreasonable for a bank to charge a lower rate of interest on a loan that is fully secured than it would for an unsecured loan.

Credit scoring

We have discussed credit scoring from time to time in this course, but we'll now examine it in more detail. Before the introduction of credit scoring techniques in the 1980s, all credit applications received by banks were manually underwritten. This meant that each application had to be scrutinised by the bank and assessed using the principles of lending which we looked at in the last section. At the end of this process, the application was either accepted or declined.

As you can imagine, this was a fairly time consuming process, depending on the complexity of the application and customers could have to wait some time to receive a decision. There was also the danger that inconsistencies in credit assessment could be manifested within the one organisation; for example, a customer could have a personal loan application declined at one branch of a bank, then make an identical application at another branch of the same bank and have their loan sanctioned!

Credit scoring has been successful in overcoming these problems as it speeds up the decision making process and ensures that consistent credit decisions are made throughout the organisation. When we match credit scoring with direct banking, it is now possible for the customer to make an application at any time of the day and receive an immediate decision.

As well as assessing credit risk, a form of credit scoring can also be used to determine what are the most suitable types of account to be offered to a particular customer wanting to open an account which has several "automatic" credit facilities attached to it.

Credit scoring was originally used for personal customers, for example mortgages, credit cards and revolving credit. However, it is now being increasingly used at the smaller end of the small to medium sized enterprises (SME) segment of the market. Credit scoring is found to be the most accurate, consistent and fair forms of credit assessment. It uses external data from credit reference agencies and information which is available within the bank on the history of the applicant and how well they have repaid credit facilities in the past. Credit scoring is a statistical means of assessing the probability of repayment of credit for an individual or small business who supplies specific data when applying for credit. The underpinning logic with credit scoring is that it is possible, by using statistics on the past performance, to predict the future credit repayment pattern of customers who have similar financial characteristics.

While credit scoring will not allow us to look into the future to determine with certainty that a particular customer will definitely repay the requested facility, it does assess the credit risk of the individual using the historical repayment record of individuals who have similar characteristics within their financial profile. Therefore, a bank can use its historic credit experience to estimate the degree of risk, be it low, medium or high. For example, statistics may show that the customer, when compared with a similarly classed customer, will behave satisfactorily at a rate of, say, 50:1. In assessing the probability of default in this way, the customers who pass the credit score set by the bank are deemed to have an acceptable default risk, whereas those applications that fall below the acceptable score set by the bank are rejected.

In the example above we are looking at a "bottom up" analysis, but it is also possible to use a "top down" analysis. With the bottom up analysis, the applicant will start with a score of, say, 500 points. Those parts of the application which have positive attributes will have points deducted from this 500, and those parts of the application deemed negative will have points added to the 500. Therefore when using the bottom up approach, a high score is regarded as "bad" and a low score is regarded as "good". The reverse is true with the top down approach, as here a high score is "bad" and a low score is "good".

The scorecard refers to the set of points that are used when scoring an application. Points are allocated according to the characteristics of various applicants whose accounts were:

- fully repaid on time with no issues

- are then compared with the characteristics of those facilities that were either slow to repay, and

- are compared again to those who did not repay their loans in full.

For example, the bank may discover that applicants who had cheques or automated payments dishonoured within the past 12 months are x% more liable to default on loans compared to those customers who did not have any items returned unpaid.

Points are then assigned to each characteristic that reflects the comparison between "good" and "slow" or "problem" loans. As you may be aware, these characteristics may range from post code to home ownership, length of time at current address, having a land line telephone, etc.

The reason for this is that if someone has defaulted on payment of a phone bill, it is likely that there will be some adverse credit information available on this person, such as a court judgement. This information could immediately filter out an application from an individual who has a poor record of paying a utility bill. On another level, if a loan is sanctioned and runs into difficulty, then having a contact number for the customer could prove invaluable.

There are several purposes for which credit scoring models can be used:

- to predict the likelihood of a new loan facility going bad or becoming delinquent

- to determine the level of credit limit that may be given to a credit card

- to predict the credit risk of approving a new current account and providing overdraft facilities.

These types of credit scoring are application scoring.

There is also behavioural scoring which can be used to:

- increase a credit card limit for an existing customer

- decide whether or not to pay items presented to an existing account if there are insufficient funds available

- upgrade credit and/or debit cards to say, a "gold" account.

The benefits of credit scoring include:

- a consistent and impartial assessment of customers – all customers are treated consistently and equitably

- allows management to control the "credit tap" – that is, increase or reduce credit exposure, therefore giving the bank control over the approval volumes/ "bad" rates

- a uniform method of processing standard customer requests

- an increase in the ability to consider volume credit approvals irrespective of value

- much improved management information systems as information is held electronically

- an efficient and cost effective method of credit assessment

- with a standard and tested system, the quality of the credit portfolio will be reliable during a stable economic cycle

- an increased level of customer service through increased response times to credit requests.

The limitations of credit scoring include:

- a large number of historical applicants and repayment patterns data is needed to build a reliable scorecard – this can present a challenge, particularly to small organisations

- it can be expensive to build and put in place, although there can be the option of developing an in-house version or buying an "off the shelf" package

- it is time sensitive, as the efficiency will deteriorate over time; old data can prove unreliable, therefore systems need to be replaced or updated over time

- it is not infallible and errors can occur

- not all lending decisions are suitable for credit scoring, depending on the customer's circumstances; it may be that some applications still need to be manually underwritten.

Lending products offered by banks

Personal lending is just as important as business lending and it is likely that the first type of lending you will encounter will be personal loans. Personal lending requires the same lending skills as for business purposes but it should be easier to build a more complete picture of the customer's income and expenditure as this is more consistent than the income and expenditure for a business. For example, a customer's salary date will be roughly the same each month, as will the dates that they pay their regular outgoings.

You should remember of course that while you will have a very good idea of your customer's present income and expenditure, the picture may change in the future. You would expect a customer's income to increase through time, but they may lose their job or their salary may contain a large commission element which may reduce in times of low business activity (such as with someone involved in sales). You should also identify how much of a salary is made up of the basic salary and how much is overtime payments which tend to be less reliable moving forward.

Lending takes many forms. Different banks have different names for their products but in practice the basic elements are broadly similar. We will now look at some of the more common lending products.

Overdrafts

Overdrafts are only available on current accounts and involve the customer withdrawing from their account, either by cheque or any other means, more than has been deposited which means that, instead of the bank being due to repay to the customer the balance on the account, the bank is owed money by the customer.

An overdraft is normally shown on a customer's statement by the abbreviation DR (meaning "debtor") after the balance of the account. Interest is charged on the outstanding debtor balance on the account and calculated on a daily basis.

Overdrafts can be granted for personal purposes, for example to assist a customer until receipt of their salary (which hopefully is mandated to the bank); or for business purposes, normally to assist a business cope with the fact that sums due from customers may not yet have been collected at the times suppliers are due to be paid. This often happens if the customer buys and sells goods on credit terms. An overdraft would not normally be granted to assist with the purchase of an asset, especially if the bank is to be repaid over a long period of time. In this case a term loan would be a more appropriate product.

A customer is normally allocated a limit up to which the account may become overdrawn. There are not usually too many terms and conditions attaching to an overdraft as overdrafts are normally repayable on demand. Given the purposes for which overdrafts are granted, it is usual to see wide fluctuations in the balance of the account which should swing into credit for periods. If the balance on the account is not fluctuating and hard core borrowing is emerging, then it may be more appropriate to grant the customer a term loan. Alternatively, it may be a sign that your customer is in some difficulty as the expected credits to the account have not been received and it may therefore be time for the bank to take some form of remedial action.

Personal loans

The minimum and maximum amounts that can be lent by way of a personal loan will vary from bank to bank. Generally, personal loans are unsecured. The maximum term is usually ten years. Personal loans can be granted for a variety of purposes, notably the purchase of motor vehicles, home improvements, holidays and purchases of household items such as furniture.

Interest is calculated by applying the rate of interest to the whole amount of the loan in respect of the full term of the loan. The total is then divided by the number of monthly payments agreed to determine the amount of the repayment instalments.

Example

A customer wishes to borrow £5,000 to purchase a motor vehicle. The loan will be repayable over a period of 5 years by monthly instalments and the bank's interest rate for personal loans is currently 10%.

(This is a simplified example and in reality the loan interest could be compounded, that is interest would be charged on the interest. If this were the case, a loan of £5,000 over 5 years, charging compound interest of 10% pa, would cost £8,052.55 or £134.22 per month.)

However, if we assume that simple interest is charged, the calculation is:

Amount of loan	£5,000
Interest (£5,000 x 10% x 5 = £500 x 5)	£2,500
Total sum repayable	£7,500
Number of repayment instalments (5 x 12)	60

The loan will therefore be repaid by 60 monthly instalments of £125.

These details will be conveyed to the customer in a credit agreement to be entered into between the bank and the customer.

A variety of personal loans are currently available on the market; for example, some will have a variable rather than a fixed rate of interest, some may allow one-off payments to be made by the customer in reduction of the debt, etc.

House purchase loans (mortgages)

This type of loan used to be provided only by building societies, but as the financial services market became more competitive in the 1980s, banks started to offer this service to customers.

At that time, it was quite a change for the banks as they were not used to committing funds for the long periods of time involved. The banks have since captured a substantial part of the house purchase loan market.

The most common types of house purchase loans are the following.

■ **Interest only mortgages**

With an interest only loan, there are no repayments to the loan account of any capital at all during the life of the loan. The payment made by the customer to the lender covers only the interested accruing on the loan. The only occurrence that will cause this amount to change is if there is a change in interest rates.

The capital sum must be repaid in its entirety at the end, therefore it is the borrower's responsibility to ensure that they have funds available at the end of the loan period to make a full repayment. They may have amassed savings over the period of the loan that would allow them to do this, but it is more common to have some form of repayment vehicle set up to allow these funds to be available.

There are three repayment vehicles which come readily to mind:

- an endowment policy

- a personal pension plan

- an ISA.

The proceeds of any of these investment products would be used to provide the borrower with a lump sum to make the capital repayment from.

The main problem is that there is no guarantee that there will be sufficient funds to make the repayment in full. You may well have read in the media that, due to the stock market performing at a lower level than was anticipated, many endowment policy holders face a shortfall when their policies mature – in other words, the proceeds of the policy will be less than the amount of the loan.

As a result, many policyholders have been advised to do one of the following:

- increase the level of premiums that they pay

- arrange to set aside additional funds to meet the shortfall

- extend the term of the loan and/or the savings policy

- convert all or part of their loan to capital and interest; by converting part of their loan to capital and interest, the amount of the loan outstanding could be reduced to the projected return from their investment.

■ **Repayment mortgages**

This type of loan requires the borrower to repay part of the capital borrowed and an interest payment charged on that capital every time an instalment is made. The balance of the account should therefore be zero at the end of the loan period.

With this arrangement, the interest repayment element makes up a larger part of the repayment than the capital element in the early stages of the loan. It is only later on in the life of the loan – when these small reductions of capital begin to reduce the total amount of capital outstanding – that the amount of interest accrued reduces and so the capital amount of the repayment becomes more dominant.

It is standard practice for lenders to look for the customer to provide some form of assurance to guarantee the repayment of the loan in the event of the borrower's death. Normally this is done by arranging for a mortgage protection policy to be put in place.

There are several benefits associated with capital and interest loans:

- they are easier for the customer to understand

- overall, repayments may be less than with an interest only loan

- it is usually possible for the customer to reduce the amount outstanding at any time by making a one-off payment into the loan account; for example, if a customer receives an annual bonus, they could pay this into the loan account and with any reduction to the amount outstanding, the monthly payments will pay off the outstanding balance of the loan more quickly

- the borrower can rest safe in the knowledge that, provided they continue to make their repayments, the loan will be fully repaid at the end of the term.

The amount of the monthly repayment will only vary as the interest rate varies. When base rate changes, there are usually illustrations in the media of how this might affect the monthly repayments of a "typical" loan. As base rate increases, so will the loan repayments, and conversely, as base rate falls, so too do the loan repayments.

■ Pension mortgages

The borrower may decide to use the tax-free lump sum element of their pension as the repayment vehicle for an interest only mortgage. With a personal pension, it is possible for the individual to retire at any age from 55 onwards. With an occupational pension scheme, this retirement age will vary with the terms of the scheme. At retirement date, the pensioner may choose to take up to 25% of the value of the pension fund as a tax-free lump sum – this lump sum can then be used to repay the mortgage.

A disadvantage to this method is that the lump sum cannot be taken until retirement, so the product is best suited to a borrower who is closer to retirement age.

There are some other disadvantages to consider:

- There is no guarantee that the lump sum will be enough to repay the mortgage – the value of the pension fund will be determined by the fund's performance

- It could be expensive to fund both the interest-only mortgage and make suitable pension contributions

- If the person moves from one pension scheme to another, the terms may vary – for example, the retirement age could be higher

- Some borrowers find these products difficult to understand

■ Muslim mortgages

As you have seen, mortgages are interest based and this is something that does not conform to Islamic Sharia law. Muslims in the UK therefore find themselves in a very difficult position as a mortgage contravenes their faith, but due to the nature of the financial services industry, if they wish to own their home, they have no choice but to reluctantly take out a mortgage. However, some providers do now provide a Sharia-compliant mortgage that is based on Ijara and Murabha methods.

Using the Ijara method:

- the financial institution purchases the property

- while the customer stays in the property, they make payments to the financial institution totalling the purchase price of the property; these payments may be scheduled over a period of up to 25 years

- during the loan repayment period, the customer is also charged rent on the property

- once the customer has repaid the money that was spent on purchasing the property, the property is sold to them.

By following this arrangement, the financial institution makes its money from the rent that the customer pays. As rent is not another name for interest, it is seen to be a fair payment for living in a property that is owned by the financial institution, rather than being a charge for borrowing money.

Using the Murabha method:

- the financial services organisation purchases the property from the seller at the original price and then sells it to the customer at a higher price

- the amount of the higher price can be paid back to the lender over a period of up to 15 years.

The financial services company will make their profit through the higher price at which they sell the property to their customer.

A major disadvantage with both these arrangements is that Stamp Duty must be paid twice in each transaction.

At present, this type of mortgage is not available from all lenders.

Whilst in the past, there were only a few mortgage products available on the market, this situation has altered over recent years, with there now being a wide range of mortgage accounts for customers to choose from – for example, fixed rate, flexible rate, capped, etc. It is beyond the scope of this course to examine all of these, but before leaving the area of mortgages, we will look at current account mortgages.

Current account mortgages

These have been recently introduced to this country but have been available abroad for many years. Here, the customer's house purchase loan and current account are amalgamated into one account.

The main advantage is that as each month's salary is credited to the account, it will reduce the total amount outstanding. As a result, the interest that is accruing on the outstanding balance is slightly lower. The cumulative effect of this over the years of the mortgage can produce savings for the customer, with the result that they can repay their loan earlier than if the mortgage and current account were maintained separately.

Normally the lender will either allow the customer to monitor the situation themselves, subject to periodic reviews by the lender, or there can be the situation where the limit on the account reduces each month in line with the mortgage repayments. In the latter situation, the customer knows, on a monthly basis, that they are on track to repay the mortgage element of the combined account.

Capital release or equity release loans

The term "equity" here refers to the difference in value between the market value of a house and the amount of borrowing secured against the house. The products in question are:

- Conventional mortgage or remortgage

- Second mortgage

- Lifetime mortgage

- Home reversion plan

You will recall that these were discussed in Chapter 2

Bridging loans

When customers move house, the settlement of the purchase and sale of the properties does not always occur on the same day and to assist, the banks offer bridging facilities to enable the customer to proceed with the purchase of the new property with the loan being repaid from the sale of the original property.

Closed bridging occurs when the date of the sale of the asset to repay the bridging has been confirmed; therefore, in a house purchase scenario, this is when there is an agreed settlement date for the sale of the property and missives have been formally concluded. The bank will thus know how much the house has been sold for and when the funds are due to be paid.

Open ended bridging covers the situation where the date of the sale of the asset to repay the bridging loan has not been agreed, in other words where the customer has bought their new property, but has not yet sold the old property. This represents a far higher risk for the bank, as they do not know when they are going to receive repayment of the bridging loan.

Although bridging loans are usually encountered when dealing with house purchase, there are other occasions when such a loan may be appropriate. For example, the customer may want to purchase a car, based on the sale proceeds of shares. However, if they need to pay for the car on 1 October, but the settlement date for the sale of the shares is not until 14

October, they will be looking for bridging finance to cover the period 1 – 14 October. This would normally be provided by an overdraft.

When agreeing a bridging loan, the bank will enter into an agreement with the customer's legal representatives to the effect that the sale proceeds of the property, less any outstanding mortgage, are remitted direct to the bank.

Term loans

These are usually granted to business customers to help buy assets such as plant and machinery where the cost involved would make it inappropriate for the borrowing to be added to the overdraft facility which should be used for working capital purposes. A term loan spreads the cost of the asset over a period – usually up to 20 years – but can be taken for longer periods with repayment instalments on a monthly, quarterly, half yearly or annual basis.

Interest on the loan usually fluctuates at a rate above the bank's base rate agreed at the outset with the customer and is debited to their operating current account. Obviously the interest paid will be high at the start of the loan but will reduce as the capital is repaid. Loans can also be at a rate which is fixed with combined capital and interest payments being made at regular intervals. The length of the term of the loan can be flexible as can the repayment arrangements including, for example, a capital holiday for, say one year to give the customer a chance to generate income from the asset to be acquired.

The terms and conditions (covenants) of the loan are normally set out in a loan agreement which will cover such things as:

- the term over which the loan is to be repaid

- the security to be granted

- conditions to be complied with by the customer, for example supply the bank with accounts at regular intervals, not grant security over any assets to any other party

- events which would render the loan immediately due for repayment (events of default) such as the customer failing to meet a repayment instalment on time, the loan being used for a different purpose to the one agreed, etc.

Overdrafts are repayable on demand, but, provided the customer stays within the conditions laid down in the loan agreement, the bank cannot demand repayment. It is usual therefore for security to be taken for such loans.

The Consumer Credit Act

This is the main piece of legislation covering consumer credit which aims to provide protection for the consumer by licensing credit providers and other organisations.

The *2006 Consumer Credit Act* reformed the *Consumer Credit Act 1974*. The *2006 Act* was a culmination of a three year review of consumer credit law and aims to protect the consumer and create a fairer and more transparent credit market by:

- enhancing consumer rights and redress by empowering consumers to challenge unfair lending, and through more effective options for resolving disputes

- improving the regulation of consumer credit businesses by streamlining the licensing system, requiring minimum standards of information provision to consumers and through targeted action to drive out rogues

- making regulation more appropriate for different types of transaction by extending protections to all consumer credit and by creating a more proportionate regime for business.

The Act defines credit as any form of financial accommodation where goods and services are sold to a buyer without any immediate payment. As such, it implies that there is trust and confidence on the part of the lender in the borrower's ability to repay in full at some future, agreed, time.

There are two types of credit agreement:

- restricted use – these apply to the acquisition of goods and services

- unrestricted use – these apply to obtaining cash loans that can be used for any purpose.

A consumer credit agreement is established where the person granting the loan (the creditor) provides the person obtaining the loan (the debtor) with credit. Previously, a "regulated" agreement was one where the credit exceeded £50 and was less than £25,000. Any loans for amounts outside these limits were exempt from the Act. However, the *Consumer Credit Act 2006* withdrew these limits with effect from April 2008.

Charge for credit and Annual Percentage Rate (APR)

The total charge for credit is the total amount that the debtor is required to pay when they take out a loan. This includes all interest and any explicit fees but does not include insurance.

The APR is the total charge, expressed as a percentage. The formulae to calculate this are laid down in the Act.

Calculating the APR can be a very complex task, but here is a simple example:

Example

Someone borrows £100 at a monthly rate of interest of 1%. It has been agreed that there will be no repayments during the first year. APR is calculated:

Loan amount	£100.00
January interest: £100 x 1% = £1 + £100	101.00
February interest: £101 x 1% = £1.01 + £101	102.01
March interest: £102.01 x 1% = £1.0201 + £102.01	103.0301
April interest:	
£103.0301x 1% = £1.030301 + £103.0301	104.0604
May interest:	
£104.0604 x 1% = £1.040604 + £104.0604	105.101
June interest:	
£105.101 x 1% = £1.05101 + £105.101	106.15201
July interest:	
£106.15201 x 1% = £1.0615201 + £106.15201	107.21353
August interest:	
£107.21353 x 1% = £1.0721353 + £107.21353	108.28566

```
September interest:
    £108.28566 x 1% = £1.0828566 + £108.28566      109.36851
October interest:
    £109.36851 x 1% = £1.0936851 + £109.36851      110.46219
November interest:
    £110.46219 x 1% = £1.1046219 + £110.46219      111.56681
December interest:
    £111.56681 x 1% = £1.1156681 + £111.56681      112.68247
Therefore the APR is 12.68%
```

Entry into credit agreements

The agreement

The Act defines the form and content of a regulated agreement. If either the debtor or the creditor do not sign the document, in its prescribed form, the agreement is not properly executed. As a result, the agreement is unenforceable without a court order. The agreement must include all the terms of the agreement, including any cancellation rights. Once the agreement has been made, a copy of the executed agreement must be sent to the debtor.

Cancellable agreements

The debtor has the right to cancel the regulated agreement within a short time after it has been executed, if any preliminary negotiations included legal representations. This is the cooling off period and does not apply if the unexecuted agreement is signed on the lender's premises or oral representations did not take place in the preliminary negotiations. If the debtor chooses to exercise these cancellation rights, the agreement is treated as if it had never existed. Therefore, all monies that the debtor has received as a result of the agreement are to be repaid to the creditor.

Other amendments to the 1974 legislation include:

- customers will now be asked to sign a separate box if they want to take out additional insurance cover along with a loan or credit card, such as payment protection insurance

- if an APR is included in an advertisement, it will always need to be more prominent than all the other financial information

- there will be a standard method for calculating the APR for credit cards; the idea behind this is to allow consumers to compare the interest rates on different cards more readily

- the charges for repaying a loan early will be restricted to interest for one month and 28 days (two months); prior to the changes in the legislation, this charge was two months and 28 days interest (three months).

Question   7

Go to question section starting on page 243

Check with the answer at the back of the book.

Review

Now consider the main learning points which were introduced in this chapter.

Go through them and tick each one when you are happy that you fully understand each point.

Then check back to the objectives at the beginning of the chapter and match them to the learning points.

Reread any section you are unsure of before moving on.

The general principles of good lending can be summarised as: the borrower, the proposition, security, repayment and remuneration.

☐

Credit scoring is a statistical means of assessing the probability of repayment of credit for an individual or small business who supplies specific data when applying for credit. By using statistics on the past performance, it is possible to predict the future credit repayment pattern of customers who have similar financial characteristics.

☐

An overdraft is a negative balance on a current account and is repayable on demand.

☐

Personal loans are (normally) unsecured loans for a fixed period of time used to finance the purchase of a specific item.

☐

A variety of mortgages are available on the market including: interest only, repayment, Sharia compliant, and fixed rate

☐

Normally associated with house purchase transactions, bridging finance is used where a major purchase has to be paid for before the customer receives funds from a major sale.

☐

A term loan is usually granted to a business to assist with the financing of an asset.

☐

The Consumer Credit Act aims to provide protection for the consumer by licensing credit providers and other organisations.

☐

 Key words in this chapter are given below. There is space to write your own revision notes and to add any other words or phrases that you want to remember.

arrangement fee

margin

canons of lending

credit scoring

cash flow projection

scorecard

application scoring

behavioural scoring

interest only mortgage

repayment mortgage

Muslim mortgage

equity release

irrevocable mandate

term loans

covenants

APR

Multiple choice questions   **7**

Try these self-test questions to assess your understanding of what you have read in this chapter.
The answers are at the back of the book.

1   A statement produced by a business borrower estimating future income and expenditure is known as which one of the following?

A   a profit and loss account

B   a cash flow statement

C   a cash flow projection

D   a debtor/creditor listing

2   Which one of the following statements is true?

A   lenders generally charge lower rates on unsecured loans than those on secured loans

B   lenders generally charge higher rates of interest on higher risk loans

C   lenders only charge arrangement fees on high risk loans

D   lenders' rates of interest are mainly determined by competitors' rates of interest

3   Eric's account balance is £2,204.56dr. What type of account does he have?

A   savings account

B   deposit account

C   current account

D   high interest investment account

Multiple choice questions   **7**

4   Which one of following is true in relation to bridging loans?

   A   banks are generally willing to offer bridging finance whether or not the borrower has sold their existing property

   B   most building societies provide bridging finance

   C   bridging finance is usually offered for short periods of time

   D   bridging finance always requires the backing of a standard security

5   Which one of the following is the main reason why banks and building societies target first time buyers for mortgage business?

   A   they tend to be more aware of the processes involved

   B   the mortgage can be set up more quickly and at lower cost

   C   there is a prospect of cross-sales over a long period of time

   D   first time buyers are a lower risk to lenders

6   Which one of the following is the main purpose of an arrangement fee?

   A   to maximise the profit from the lending transaction

   B   to pay any legal bills incurred by the customer

   C   to act as a cash buffer in the event of default on the loan

   D   to cover the bank's costs in setting up the loan

Multiple choice questions   **7**

7   Which one of the following would not be taken into account when considering a lending proposition?

A   the borrower's financial acumen

B   the nationality of the borrower

C   the age of the borrower

D   the maturity of the borrower

8 Securities for Advances

Objectives

By the end of this chapter, you should be able to:

- Explain why a bank takes security.

- Differentiate between direct and third party security.

- Describe the attributes of a good security.

- Describe the main forms of security encountered in banks, namely: guarantees, standard securities, assignation of life policies, pledge of marketable securities, bonds and floating charges, cash deposits.

- Explain what is meant by the discharge of security.

Introduction

By now you will be aware that any decision by a bank to lend money to a customer will depend on that customer's ability to repay, but in a great many cases, even where a bank is satisfied as to a customer's ability to repay, it will look for security to be granted in its favour. In this chapter we'll look at the main reasons why a bank takes security, the attributes of a good security and at some of the more common types and features of security taken by a bank.

Why does a bank take security?

As previously discussed, it is not customary for a bank to lend to a customer unless it is completely satisfied that the advance, whether by way of loan, overdraft or otherwise, will be repaid from the customer's resources. In other words, the banker must be satisfied by the viability of the proposal.

It is not normal practice to lend to a customer where the decision is based largely on the value of the security offered, that is, a bank's agreement to lend should depend on its view of the customer's current and future ability to repay. Although consideration will be given to the need for security, it should not be regarded as an alternative source of repayment. That said, it is still the case that the availability of security is a crucial factor to be considered by the bank in deciding whether or not to lend the money as there is always an element of risk. For example, a customer may lose their job and have insufficient income to repay the bank loan or the customer's business may not bring in the amount of money predicted in the cash flow forecast, or worse, the business may fail and the customer may be declared bankrupt.

It's perhaps useful to think of the banker as a trapeze artist. When the trapeze artist is performing his act, he does not do so thinking that at any moment he is about to fall, but there is always a possibility that this will happen – hence a safety net. Security fulfils a similar role as the safety net for the banker. A loan should never be made if the banker feels that the only way to obtain repayment will be to realise the security. However, unforeseen circumstances could conspire to make it difficult, if not impossible, for the customer to make repayment – hence the need for security. It allows the banker to sleep more easily at night!

We looked at limited companies earlier and you should remember that a director of a company is not personally liable for the company's debts; therefore there is always a risk that the company may go into liquidation with insufficient assets to repay bank borrowing. In short, a bank looks for security in an attempt to protect itself against unforeseen circumstances and the possibility of the customer becoming insolvent.

In the event of a company being unable to pay its debts, its creditors will be entitled to rank on the assets of the company in the following order:

1. Secured creditors
2. Insolvency fees
3. Preferential creditors
4. Floating charge holders
5. Unsecured creditors
6. Interest on preferential or ordinary debts
7. Deferred debts, such as loans from subsidiary companies
8. Shareholders

You can see from this how important it is that a bank holds security and that the security is properly constituted.

Some of the more common types of security are:

- guarantee

- security over a dwelling house

- security over a shop, warehouse or factory

- assignation of a life policy

- pledge of marketable securities (stocks and shares)

- bond and floating charge (can only be granted by a company)

- pledge of a cash deposit.

There are other types of security available to a bank, such as a mortgage over a fishing vessel, security over produce, an assignation of interest in a trust estate, but here we will consider only the above types which are the ones that are more likely to arise on a day-to-day basis.

Direct security and third party security

Direct security is security granted by the borrower for their own obligations whereas third party security is provided by someone other than the borrower but is available for the borrower's obligations (but not necessarily the obligations of the party granting the security – much will depend on how the security deed is drawn).

The distinction between direct security and third party security is important as in the event of the insolvency of a customer if direct security is realised (that is, if a bank takes steps to convert its security into cash) and the proceeds are applied in repayment of the customer's debt, part of the customer's estate has gone towards repayment of the debt; therefore the bank must deduct the value of the security from its claim against the customer's estate. If the security held is third party security, its value does not require to be deducted from the customer's debt; therefore the bank would not be required to claim a reduced amount from the estate of the customer.

Example

A bank holds security worth £50,000 for a customer's debt of £100,000. The customer is declared bankrupt and it has been agreed that all creditors will receive a dividend of £0.50 per £1.00 of debt.

If the security held is direct security, the situation will be:

Amount of debt	£100,000
Less value of security	£ 50,000
Amount of claim	£ 50,000
Dividend paid (50,000 x £0.50)	£ 25,000
Loss to the bank	£ 25,000

If the security held is third party security, the situation will be:

Amount of debt (therefore amount of claim)	£100,000
Dividend paid (100,000 x £0.50)	£ 50,000
	£ 50,000
Value of security	£ 50,000
Loss to the bank	Nil

You can see therefore that third party security is of greater benefit to the bank than security provided by the customer.

Attributes of a good security

Now that you understand why a bank takes security, we'll look at what attributes a good security should have. So that the bank can rely on security provided, it must be fully enforceable and should be able to withstand challenge by the borrower or one of the other creditors. The bank should also know at all times how much the security is worth and its value should not decrease before it can be relied upon.

The following three attributes are important when considering security:

- simplicity of title

- stability of value

- realisability.

It may be that the various items of security we are about to consider will not possess all of the good attributes as there is an argument that there is no such thing as the perfect banking security, but the merits of each form of security may be judged according to the following.

Simplicity of title

It is important to both the bank and its customer that the security can be completed easily and cheaply. It should be relatively easy to ascertain that the person proposing to grant the security is able to do so and, if security is to be granted over an asset, the asset is actually owned by them.

This attribute is present in most forms of security although in the case of a security to be granted over a property of some description, such as a dwelling house or a shop, it is sometimes necessary for the ownership of the property to be investigated by checking the title deeds. This will almost always be undertaken by lawyers acting on behalf of the bank. Ideally, the title to the subject of a security should be free from all liabilities or anything that may prevent the bank from dealing with the security as it sees fit.

Stability of value

It is vitally important that a bank can rely on the value that it has placed on the security at the time it agrees to lend to the customer and that the value of the security will not fall during the currency of the advance so that, if the customer is unable to repay the sum borrowed, the bank will be repaid in full by realising the security. For this reason it is a good idea when calculating how much cover is provided by security to allow a margin as a safeguard against fluctuations in value.

There are several reasons why a bank will choose to discount the value of a security, including:

- the value of the security may fall from time to time, therefore the bank may wish to build in a contingency against the value of the security being lower at the time of realisation than the value at the time the advance was agreed

- if the bank has to realise the security, there could be associated expenses, therefore the bank would want to have these costs covered from the proceeds of the realisation of the security

- if the security has to be realised, the customer may well have been having financial difficulties and so has not been able to meet the ongoing interest charges on the borrowing – these may be added to the outstanding obligation; consequently, the final debt that the customer owes the bank may be greater than the amount of the outstanding borrowing; again, the bank would want to guard against possible loss by having a margin on the underlying value of the security.

The level of discount is normally expressed as a percentage; for example, for security purposes, residential property is usually valued at 80% of market value. These percentages may vary from time to time and may be different from one bank to another. You should therefore check what the current security discount values are in your bank.

Finally, the value of the security should also be easily ascertainable; for example, the price of shares is given in many daily newspapers or on websites.

Realisability

You should always remember that, if the worst comes to the worst and converting the security to cash is the only option left for the bank to recover its money, it is of the utmost importance that the bank is able to realise its security quickly and without undue formality. Any delay is likely to increase the risk of the debt and/or the interest accruing thereon not being repaid in full.

Not all security held by the bank will be quickly realisable. For example, the bank may hold a security over a dwelling house owned by the customer but the house is let out to a third party who may enjoy certain rights of occupation and the bank would not be able to sell the house unless the sale was subject to the tenant's rights. This means that the new owner of the house could not live there but would receive the rental monies paid by the tenant. The existence of the tenant's rights will probably mean that there are fewer people willing to purchase the house than would have been the case if the bank were able to offer vacant possession, therefore it may take longer to sell the house and/or the price obtained may not be as high.

Types of security

Guarantee

A guarantee is an undertaking by one party to answer for the debt or default of another person. A guarantee differs from other types of security in that it does not by itself provide the bank with any security rights or an asset with which it can deal; for example, if the bank held security over shares it can sell the shares on realising its security. This is not the case with a guarantee. If the customer is unable to repay the debt, the only action that can be taken as regards the guarantor is for the bank to demand payment from him. If the guarantor is unable or unwilling to meet his obligations in terms of the guarantee, the bank is in much the same position as it would have been had it lent to the customer on an unsecured basis.

In such circumstances it would be necessary for the bank to raise an action against the person who has granted the guarantee.

It is possible for the bank to mitigate this risk by taking additional security over an asset held by the guarantor. For example, it could be that the guarantor has a portfolio of shares that the bank could take security over. In this situation, should the bank have to realise the guarantee, they have the comfort of knowing that they also have title to the guarantor's shares which they can sell should the guarantor not pay up under the terms of the guarantee.

The three parties to a guarantee are:

1   the person who has granted the guarantee, undertaking to make payment – the guarantor or the cautioner or the surety

2   the party in whose favour the guarantee has been granted – the creditor or lender

3   the person whose obligations have been guaranteed – the debtor or the principal debtor or the primary obligant.

A guarantee will not provide the bank with a tangible security nor any asset to dispose of and is therefore only as good as the person granting it. Unless the guarantor has the means to meet his obligations, the guarantee could be worthless. It is for this reason that it is essential in all cases to carry out checks that the guarantor, if called upon to do so, could implement his guarantee obligation. As we have just discussed, in a great many cases, the bank will require the guarantee to be supported by some form of first party security from the guarantor. Later we will look at security over stocks and shares and over property which can be granted in support of a guarantee, which is a third party security as the guarantee obligation is a first party obligation as far as the guarantor is concerned.

On the basis that the guarantor is financially sound and reliable and/or the guarantee is fully supported by tangible security, the security can be constituted easily and cheaply. While at the time a guarantee is granted the guarantor may appear to be financially strong, this position may deteriorate during the lifetime of the guarantee, so it is essential to continually monitor the guarantor's circumstances. For example, if the guarantor is not a customer of the bank, it is likely that, at the time the guarantee is contemplated, the guarantor will be asked to provide details of income and expenditure, to be confirmed by the guarantor's bankers and initiating a status enquiry which should be updated on an annual or biannual basis.

It has been said that a guarantee is the easiest form of security to constitute but the most difficult to realise. This is because few guarantors, when they sign a guarantee, expect to be called upon to make payment. Often therefore, a demand from the bank to make payment under the guarantee will come as a complete shock to the guarantor and if there is some way round having to make payment you can be sure that the guarantor, or at least his solicitor, will look for it! The banker must ensure therefore that any possible loopholes are closed. For this reason, a guarantee should always take the form of the bank's standard guarantee document.

The most obvious defence open to a guarantor is that he did not fully appreciate what he was signing or that he was coerced into signing the guarantee by the bank which must always therefore exercise great care in all its dealings with the proposed guarantor, especially during the preliminary negotiations. Basically the bank should always request the borrower to obtain a suitable guarantee and make the necessary arrangements for the granting of the guarantee. The bank should take great care not to become involved in any preliminary negotiations with the proposed guarantor because if the guarantor were to be able to plead at a later date that he was induced to grant the guarantee by the influence of the bank, he might be able to escape liability and the bank would lose the benefit of the security. We will look at this concept of undue influence shortly.

The bank, however, may be asked one or two questions by a prospective guarantor as to the financial condition and the prospects of the borrower. In such circumstances the bank has to balance its duty of confidentiality to its customer with its obligation not to misrepresent the facts to the guarantor and thereby put the validity of the guarantee at risk.

The safest course of action open to the bank is to have a meeting with the prospective guarantor and the borrower both present, or to obtain the written authority of the borrower to disclose information to the proposed guarantor. Either way, during the course of discussions with the guarantor the banker should not disclose any information that is not specifically requested and make the responses strictly factual. The banker must however guard against misrepresenting the facts to the guarantor by remaining silent when it is obvious from a comment made by the guarantor that he is labouring under a misapprehension about the borrower's affairs.

The concept of undue influence has been with us for centuries and applies where a stronger party, as a matter of law or provable from prevailing circumstances, induces a weaker party to enter into a contract where he or she would not otherwise do so. The courts will usually be willing to set such a contract aside when the weaker party claims that they would not have entered into the contract if they had realised and understood the pressure being levied upon them to do so. Nevertheless, the courts will be unwilling to set aside the contract where the weaker party has received a benefit from the contract: National Westminster Bank PLC -v- Morgan, 1985.

Within the legal framework, in general, there are certain defined relationships, where it would be presumed that undue influence had taken place, such as doctor/patient, parent/child, solicitor/client, guardian/ward, religious adviser/disciple and trustee/beneficiary – the stronger party being the first one, when a contract had been entered into, unless evidence could be produced to make the court decide otherwise. In other relationships, such as child/parent, husband/wife: Howes -v- Bishop, 1909, Bank of Montreal -v- Stuart, 1911 and engaged couples: Zemet -v- Hyman, 1961, there would be a need for the weaker party, based on prevailing circumstances, to prove that undue influence took place, thereby enabling the contract to be set aside.

The following illustrations will show how involvement can arise.

Case study

1

Consider the case where a guarantee has been entered into by the weaker party who is not well versed in financial matters, and the security has been taken to secure the liabilities of one person (subsequently shown to be the "stronger" person) owed to a bank. In these circumstances, as undue influence would be presumed to have taken place, the bank's security may be held to be unenforceable, thereby resulting in the bank's advance being unsecured.

2

A bank may be considering taking a security over property owned jointly by a husband and wife to secure the liabilities to the bank of, say, the husband. It would be possible for the wife to claim that she did not enter into the security of her own free will and, as such, the security could be considered as void and set aside. If such a plea were to succeed, the bank would be holding unenforceable security.

> **3**
>
> A bank itself could be accused of exercising undue influence. This may arise where the person giving the security, and the person whose liabilities are being secured, both maintain accounts with the same bank. If this happened, the bank has a clear conflict of interests and it could be argued that the bank, however subtly, wanted some form of security and "influenced" one party into giving such security.

To all intents and purposes, the only way banks can totally prevent any plea of undue influence succeeding is to insist that independent legal advice is always taken by the guarantor from his/her own solicitor. In the case of O'Hara -v- Allied Irish Banks and Another, 1984 it was held that where a prospective guarantor is not a customer of the bank, there is no duty of care on the bank to explain the nature and effect of the contract of security being entered into, nor the maximum claim the bank can make thereunder. However, where the prospective guarantor is a customer of the bank, it has been held that the bank, because it has a duty of care to that person, should insist on independent legal advice where the prospective guarantor is:

- not well versed financially, or

- vulnerable to the pressure of the principal debtor, or

- charging the bulk of his financial assets as security, or

- normally relies upon the bank for financial advice.

From time to time, after the guarantee has been signed, the guarantor may ask the bank to tell him how the borrower's account stands. Again the banker must exercise caution and confine his answer to something along the lines of "Your liability in terms of your guarantee presently stands at £ …". If the balance on the borrower's account is greater than the amount of the guarantee, the banker would reply "Your guarantee is being fully relied upon at present."

If two or more guarantors grant a guarantee, they are jointly and severally liable for payment of the guarantee obligation. We looked at this concept earlier in the course and you will remember that joint and several liability means that each party is liable for the full amount of the obligation.

Case study

The bank is proposing to lend the sum of £20,000 to James Wilson provided that Mr Wilson can arrange for a suitable guarantee to be granted in favour of the bank. Two days later Mr Wilson advises the bank that two of his friends, Brian Johnstone and Elaine Smith, have agreed to grant a guarantee. The bank carries out checks and is satisfied as to the means of both intending guarantors, but Mr Johnstone does not seem to have the same amount of wealth as Mrs Smith and she seems to be in a more secure job.

If the bank were to take two guarantees for £10,000 each, one from Brian Johnstone and one from Elaine Smith, the most they could recover from Mrs Smith would be £10,000, even if by that time Mr Johnstone was no longer able to meet his obligations.

If the bank had taken a joint and several guarantee for £20,000 from Mrs Smith and Mr Johnstone, then it would have been able to recover the whole £20,000 from Mrs Smith.

A standard bank guarantee contains a great number of important clauses which we will not be examining here, but you should appreciate that each clause in a guarantee has a specific purpose and any request by a prospective guarantor to amend or delete any of the clauses in a standard bank guarantee should be referred to the specialist department responsible for security for advances or to legal advisers, depending on the practice of the particular bank.

Security over Land and Property

Security over property (land, land with buildings on it, leases, etc.) is constituted by way of a mortgage deed.

Fisher and Lockwood's "Law of Mortgage" defines a mortgage as:

> **"a form of security created by contract, conferring an interest in property defeasible upon performing the condition of paying a given sum of money, with or without interest, or of performing some other condition."**

There are three key aspects of a mortgage contained in this definition:

- a mortgage is a contract and therefore is subject to the general law of contract

- contracts need not be in writing, though in the case of land, they usually are

- a mortgage is an undertaking by the borrower (the mortgagor) according to the conditions of the contract; thus it is the mortgagor/borrower who gives the mortgage, i.e. the borrower provides the security.

The Law of Property Act 1925 is the main piece of legislation governing land ownership in England and Wales. This Act greatly simplified the ways in which mortgages could be created. The most common method is to use a contract called a legal charge where the purchaser of the property legally owns it as soon as the mortgage deed (document) is signed – hence the term "owner-occupier". However, a further right is created in favour of the lender, meaning that the lender has a series of rights (including possession and power of sale) if the borrower fails to honour the terms of the contract.

The creation or transfer of rights over land is called a conveyance; thus, when a mortgage deed is executed, there are two conveyances:

- the transfer of the property from the vendor to the purchaser

- the creation of rights in favour of the lender (mortgagee).

Most mortgages are executed using a legal charge which usually consists of a single page document that binds the borrower and the lender to specified terms. Both the borrower and the lender have rights and duties, or liabilities, under the mortgage. These are known collectively as mortgage covenants or mortgage clauses. Many such covenants or clauses will appear in every mortgage deed and are generally known as "standard conditions".

The covenant for payments is an obvious one as the mortgage will provide for the repayment of capital and interest on a regular basis, or on an interest only basis, with the capital repaid at the end of the mortgage term.

Examples of other standard conditions include requirements for the borrower to:

- keep the property in good repair

- allow the lender access for inspection

- not make structural alterations without the lender's consent

- insure the property in accordance with the lender's requirements

- not to let the property out without the lender's permission.

Some lenders use mortgage deeds that consolidate the repayment obligations of borrowers across the whole range of loan accounts held. These are all moneys deeds. The obvious benefit to the lender is that the security for the mortgage can be realised in the event of default on any borrowings, such as an overdraft or personal loan.

The mortgage deed will provide that the whole debt will become immediately payable if, for example:

- any of the borrower's covenants are breached

- arrears amounting to a specified number of monthly instalments are due but unpaid

- the borrower becomes bankrupt

- the property is compulsorily purchased.

Once the debt becomes due in any of the above circumstances, the lender can:

- take possession of the property and manage it

- agree to the letting of the property

- make repairs and improvements to protect the value of the security

- appoint a receiver to manage the property and use the moneys collected to reduce the mortgage debt

- sell the property in possession.

Completion of the security

To initiate the completion of security the bank must instruct solicitors to act in the drawing up of a mortgage. This cost is paid by the borrower and is often one objection made by borrowers when they are requested to grant a mortgage.

In addition to the solicitor's fees, there will be other fees and costs including, for example, the fees for registering the security at HM Land Registry, carrying out a search of the Local Land Charges Register to see if there are any local planning issues, and VAT. To avoid any potential conflict of interest, it could be preferable for separate solicitors to act for the borrower and for the bank. However, the fees will be greater than if the same solicitors act and therefore, in most cases, the same solicitors will act for both the borrower and the bank.

Land registration has been compulsory for all transfers of land since 1990 which means that eventually every piece of land in the country will be registered, although unregistered land remains as such until it changes hands. This process towards universal registration is a long one because some land is rarely, if ever, transferred; for example, land belonging to national and local government.

For registered land, HM Land Registry holds details on three registers:

- property register – details the land, title number and a plan

- proprietorship (ownership) register – includes the name and address of the property and owner, the nature of title and date of registration

- charges register – includes, for example, any charges over the property and spouse's interests under the Family Law Act 1996.

Unregistered land is that which has yet to be transferred since the introduction of compulsory registration in 1990. If land is unregistered, then no details of the property and ownership will have been registered in the Property and Proprietorship Registers at HM Land Registry. This information will still be contained in the title deeds, while any charges and other rights over the property will be registered in the Land Charges Register.

Once they are instructed by the bank to act in the drawing up of the mortgage deed, the lawyers will conduct searches in the Property, Proprietorship and Charges Registers in the case of registered land. If the land is unregistered, the title deeds will be checked to confirm details of the property and title and the Land Charges Register will be searched to confirm whether there are any charges or registration of third party interests in the property.

Other searches will also need to be undertaken to ensure, for example, that the land offered as security is not common land and that the prospective borrower is not an undischarged bankrupt.

On the basis that the searches do not disclose any adverse information of which the solicitors and the bank were unaware, the lawyers will proceed to complete the mortgage deed and have it executed by the grantor.

The bank will want to ensure that they have an enforceable security. Information on this is provided by the lawyer on a form known as a Certificate of Title. On receipt of this certificate, certain checks must be undertaken by the bank, including:

- the property details are correct

- the certificate relates to the correct customer

- the certificate has been prepared on the bank's standard form

- the solicitor's signature is present

- the certificate is dated

- the certificate has been completed in full

- there are no onerous conditions warranting further investigation

- if a qualified certificate has been received, this should be referred to the bank's legal department

- the formal offer letter received has been signed and dated by all relevant parties and witnessed by a non-family member

- all outstanding conditions laid down in the offer letter have been fully satisfied.

It is also extremely important to bear in mind that prior to releasing any funds, a final check should be instigated in order to confirm that all outstanding conditions stipulated in the original offer document have been completed in full. If this is not the case, the facility should not be released.

Although the security can now be considered as covering the obligations, it is not yet fully completed. The solicitors still require to send the deed to HM Land Registry for registration. Although mortgage deeds are recorded/ registered on the date of receipt by the bank, the actual registration process at HM Land Registry may still take some time.

At the end of the transaction, the mortgage deed, the title deeds and results of searches will be delivered to the bank.

Postponed mortgage deeds

Generally speaking, a bank does not like to lend against a property over which security already exists in favour of another lender. However, you will undoubtedly come across situations where this occurs.

Examples

The house that you currently live in has a mortgage deed/standard security in place to the bank or building society from whom you have a mortgage. Let's say that your house has a market value of £150,000, with your mortgage being £50,000. You have decided that you want to build an extension and approach another lender. You may find that the other lender is willing to grant the facility and will take a subsequent mortgage deed/standard security over your home.

If a second loan is made on a property, repayment of that loan is postponed in favour of the first one. The problem is that the first lender may call up the debt and the security at any time without consulting the second lender. Occasionally, you may find the second lender is willing to advance funds to pay off the original mortgage in order to obtain a first ranking security.

When dealing with a subsequent mortgage deed, confirmation should be obtained from the prior security holder(s) that they have no objection to the mortgage deed being granted in favour of the second lender before proceeding with the constitution of the security. When the bank's security has been completed, intimation of the security will require to be given to the prior security holders who should be asked to confirm the amount of the facility that they have outstanding. At the same time, the prior security holders should be asked for confirmation that they are not obliged to make any further advances under the contract to which their security relates.

If a bank holds security and receives intimation that a second security has been granted in favour of another party, the first security is limited to advances outstanding at the date of intimation along with interest present and future on these advances. Operations on the account should therefore be stopped at once if intimation of a second security is received, as any future advances made will be postponed to the second security.

Assignation of a life policy

A life policy is a contract to pay a cash sum on the occurrence of a specified event or the elapse of an agreed period of time in return for the payment of a premium. For example, in return for a premium which may be paid monthly, annually or in a single instalment, a life assurance company will pay a cash sum to the person paying the premium (the policyholder) on the survival of the policyholder until, say, their sixtieth birthday. Alternatively, the contract may be to pay a sum to the relatives of the policyholder in the event of the policyholder's death.

An individual will take out a policy of insurance with a life assurance company for a variety of reasons – perhaps looking for a means of investment, in which case they will take out an endowment policy entitling the policyholder to a share in the profits of the life assurance company, or wishing to protect their survivors in the event of their death during a specified period, for example during the duration of a mortgage, in which case they will arrange a term assurance policy. They may wish to provide for their survivors in the event of their death whenever that occurs, in which case a whole life policy is the appropriate product.

The person who arranges the policy and becomes responsible for payment of the premiums is the proposer. The person who is to be paid the proceeds of the policy is the beneficiary. Often the proposer and the beneficiary are the same person. The person who is the subject of the contract, that is, on whose death and/or survival the policy proceeds are to be paid, is the life assured. Often the proposer, the beneficiary and the life assured are the same person! The assurer is the life assurance company which issues the policy and undertakes to pay out the sum assured in return for the premiums.

Question   **8**

Go to question section starting on page 243

Check with the answer at the back of the book.

How a bank can be granted security over a life policy

Security over a life policy is taken by way of an assignation in security which is granted by the policyholder (the proposer) in favour of the bank. The assignation is granted in favour of the bank in consideration of sums due and to become due to the bank (that is, it is normally an "all monies" deed). In terms of the assignation, the bank is entitled to be paid the proceeds of the policy on maturity.

The bank is also given the power to sell or surrender the policy. The surrender value of a policy is the amount that the insurance company will be entitled to pay out to cancel the policy. It is normally only endowment types of policies that acquire surrender values; term policies and whole life policies do not acquire surrender values as, in the case of a term policy, on maturity there is no sum payable by the insurance company and with whole life policies the insurance company cannot say how much longer the insurance policy will run. The surrender value of a policy is often considerably less than the maturity value, although much will depend on the term remaining until the agreed maturity date of the policy; that is, if a policy is taken out for a period of twenty years you would expect the surrender value after two years to be considerably less than the surrender value after eighteen years.

An alternative to surrendering the policy would be for the bank to sell the policy to one of the specialised companies who deal in this market.

The bank should obtain the original policy from the proposed grantor of the assignation, and the details of the insurance company, policy number, amount, date, etc of the policy should be detailed in the assignation deed. Most banks will have different requirements as to how much of the policy details are repeated in the assignation.

There are no hard and fast rules. Basically there should be sufficient details in the assignation to identify the policy and distinguish it from any other policy. On this basis the assignation should contain as a minimum the name of the insurance company and the policy number.

Having taken an assignation of the policy it is obviously important that the insurance company is aware that the policy has been assigned so that the bank can collect the maturity proceeds of the policy or surrender/sell it. To achieve this, the bank intimates the assignation of the policy to the insurance company and seeks the following confirmations:

- that the insurance company acknowledges the assignation and will be prepared to act accordingly

- that the policy has not already been assigned

- that the premiums are paid up to date

- that the insurance company itself does not have a claim on the policy.

As the bank's security is wholly dependent on the policy remaining in force, it is essential that the premiums are paid up to date as the policy may be cancelled due to non payment. The banker should therefore make regular checks to ensure that the premiums are being paid up to date. Most premiums are collected by way of direct debit or standing order so it should be easy to check the customer's account that the premiums are being paid up to date.

Case study

The bank is experiencing some difficulty with its customer, William Farmer, and is concerned at the level of his overdraft which is presently £45,000. The only security held is an assignation of a policy which will mature in 18 months time. The estimated maturity value of the policy is £50,000, but the current surrender value of the policy is only £25,000.

The bank has written to Mr Farmer advising that he should take steps to reduce the level of his overdraft and that it will not permit any further debits to the account until he has paid in at least £15,000.

The following day, a direct debit for £25 is due to be paid to The Scottish Friendly Assurance Company. Notwithstanding what the bank said to Mr Farmer, it would be inadvisable for the bank to return the direct debit unpaid as to do so could result in the life policy being cancelled and therefore affecting the value of the bank's security.

An assignation may be granted as direct security or as third party security, although in cases where it is being granted to secure the obligations of third parties, it is often preferable to take a guarantee from the assignor and to hold the assignation in support of the assignor's guarantee obligation. In this way the assignation will also be available for the assignor's own obligations to the bank (if any).

Question   9

Go to question section starting on page 243

Check with the answer at the back of the book.

Pledge of marketable securities

Marketable securities are commonly called stocks and shares. A bank may be granted security over shares in a company, although unless the shares in the company are bought and sold on a recognised stock exchange it may be difficult, if not impossible, for the bank to sell them if the need ever arose. The prices of shares quoted on the Stock Exchange can fluctuate widely, especially at the time of the company's results or if there are rumours of a takeover bid or merger. You will appreciate therefore that a security over shares does not possess at least one of the attributes of a good security – stability of value. The price of shares is quite easy to obtain as they are quoted in most national newspapers, in the *Financial Times*, on the internet or by contacting a stockbroker.

Looking at the price of a share either in the financial pages of a newspaper, or online, there are two points to remember:

- the price quoted is a mid market price

- the price may already be out of date.

Two prices are usually quoted – the selling price and the buying price. For example, the share price of Multinational Conglomerates PLC may be 103p - 108p which means that a buyer can buy shares for £1.08 each and a seller sell shares for £1.03 each. The price quoted in the newspapers or on online for this particular share would probably be 105p. The price in the paper will also be the closing price for the previous day's trading, so that if you see the share price in the newspaper at say, 11am on a Monday morning, this is the mid-market price of the share when trading finished on the previous Friday evening and the shares will already have been traded for around three hours on the Monday morning.

A share in a company also has two values – nominal value and market value. The nominal value of a share is the value which the company put on the shares when they were issued and the market value is the value of the share on the Stock Exchange. For example, a company may issue shares of 25p each, if the shares are traded on the Stock Exchange the value of the shares may be more than 25p, they may also be less!

The nominal value of a share has no bearing at all on its market value which reflects the supply and demand for the shares on the market. The views of investors will influence this value; for example, what they think the company is actually worth and whether or not they consider the company has good prospects. It is quite possible for a company share to have a nominal value of 10p and a market value of, say, £4.50.

When lending to a customer against the security of shares, it is advisable to allow a reasonable margin for fluctuations in value. It is also preferable to obtain a security over a diverse portfolio of shares if possible rather than the shares of one company only, that is, do not put all your eggs in one basket! It is also worth remembering that the lower the share price, the greater the impact will be of a 1p movement in the share price. It is for these reasons that banks will normally heavily discount the value of shares held in security – sometimes even valuing the security at nil.

Case study

A bank is lending to two customers, Mr Smith and Mrs Brown.

Mr Smith
Overdraft: £ 57,000
Security: 150,000 shares in ABC plc of 10p each
Current market value 40p   £ 60,000

Mrs Brown
Overdraft: £200,000
Security: 72,000 shares in DEF plc of 25p each
Current market value £3.50   £252,000

If the share price of ABC plc falls by just 3p, the value of the shareholding (£55,500) will be less than the amount owing to the bank, whereas the share price of DEF plc can fall by over 70p and the advance would still be covered by the value of the shareholding (72,000 @ £2.79 = £200,880). You should also keep in mind that were the bank looking to realise this security and clear either of these overdrafts, there would still be accrued interest to apply to these accounts, thus increasing the amount of the overdraft.

This case underlines two important principles when lending against the security of shares:

- always allow a sizeable margin for fluctuations in share prices

- if possible, take security over a portfolio of shares rather than the shares of one company only.

How the security is constituted

When someone buys shares in a company, their name is noted in a register of members which is maintained by the company or by its registrars. As evidence of ownership of the shares, the holder of the shares will normally receive a share certificate which is needed when the shares are sold. As a first step therefore, the bank should obtain the share certificate or other document of title from the customer.

It is not enough, however, just to hold the certificate and do nothing else – a bank will not be able to sell shares if the name on the share certificate and in the company's register is that of one of its customers. A certificate will therefore have to be issued in the bank's name and the bank to be shown in the company's register as the owner of the shares.

In practice, as strictly speaking the shares to be secured will remain the property of the customer, and to distinguish shares held by a bank as security from shares held as an investment, the shares are transferred into the name of a company set up specifically to hold shares pledged to the bank. Such a company is a nominee company and is shown in the company's register as the "shareholder"; however, the customer will be entitled to the dividends and to cast their vote at general meetings of the company.

To complete the security, the customer will normally be asked to execute a letter of pledge. Every bank will have its own style of letter of pledge which provides evidence that the shares in question have actually been secured to the bank and that the bank is empowered to sell the shares in the event of the customer not meeting their liabilities to the bank when called upon to do so.

Bond and floating charge

A bond and floating charge can only be granted by a company and, as the name suggests, the charge does not attach to any particular company asset. For example, if a company owned a property and granted a bond and floating charge to a bank, the existence of the charge would not be registered in the Land Registry. Similarly, if the company owned shares, the shares would not be transferred into the name of the bank's nominee company.

Once a company has granted a bond and floating charge in favour of a bank, it is still free to deal with its assets in the ordinary course of business, although most charges contain a prohibition on the company disposing of assets not in the ordinary course of business.

A bond and floating charge empowers the holder to appoint a receiver who will look after the interests of the bond and floating chargeholder and either sell off assets of the company to repay the chargeholder or continue trading with a view to finding a buyer for the whole business as a going concern. It is when a bank appoints a receiver that the bond and floating charge attaches specifically to the assets owned by the company at the time. When this happens the charge is said to crystallise.

All companies must be registered with the Registrar of Companies. Each company must also maintain a Register of Charges with the Registrar and all charges granted by a company must be registered within twenty-one days of being created. A bond and floating charge is created when it is executed by the company.

In most banks bonds and floating charges are prepared by a central specialist department which will also attend to the registration of the charge. It is therefore important that executed bonds and floating charges are returned to this department as soon as possible so that the charge may be registered within the twenty-one day period.

It is possible for a company to grant bonds and floating charges in favour of two or more lenders. The charges take priority in the order in which they are registered and when the creation of a subsequent bond and floating charge is intimated to a lender they should stop operations on any fluctuating overdraft to preserve their position, and prevent the rule in Clayton's Case operating against the bank. Again it is possible for two or more lenders to enter into a ranking agreement to regulate the ranking of their bonds and floating charges.

It is also possible to use such an agreement to regulate the ranking of fixed charges and bonds and floating charges, although the general rule is that a fixed charge takes priority over a bond and floating charge, regardless of when they were executed and registered.

Pledge of a cash deposit

If you think back to the attributes of a good security, a security over a cash deposit must be one of the few items of security that possess all of the attributes. If the deposit to be pledged is lodged with the bank and the depositor signs a letter of pledge securing the deposit to the bank and empowering the bank to uplift the funds and apply them in reduction or repayment of the secured debt, that security has simplicity of title as it is clear, without lengthy investigation, to whom the funds belong and the security can be constituted easily and cheaply. The cash deposit will not fluctuate in value therefore it has stability of value (leaving aside the argument that through time, inflation will erode the value of cash) and its value is readily ascertainable. The security will also be realisable as the bank can easily transfer the deposit from one account to the secured debt.

The cash deposits are normally provided by a third party, either as direct security or in support of a guarantee, although sometimes the borrower has funds which are kept separate from the business accounts and the bank may wish to prevent the customer from uplifting these funds while indebted to the bank.

Normally the deposit is placed in an interest bearing account and the depositor is asked to sign a letter of pledge authorising the bank to hold the funds in security for the particular purpose and to uplift and apply them if need be. It is sometimes considered desirable to hold a signed withdrawal request with the completed letter of pledge.

If the deposit is lodged with a building society or another bank and the building society permits the sums in the account to be pledged (it is not possible to obtain a pledge over funds lodged in an ISA – the funds would normally be transferred into the name of the bank's nominee company) a letter of pledge would be taken.

Discharge of security

Often all that is required to discharge security is for the bank to confirm in writing that it is no longer looking to the item of security for the obligations of the customer. This is what would happen in the case of a guarantee or a letter of pledge in respect of a cash deposit, although in some cases a bank may actually return a cancelled guarantee to the former guarantor.

In the case of a pledge of marketable securities, the bank can advise the person who has pledged the shares that the letter of pledge has been cancelled or return the cancelled letter of pledge, depending on the practice of the individual bank; however, it will be necessary to transfer "ownership" of the shares from the nominee company to the name of the beneficial owner of the shares.

In Scotland, a bank discharges a standard security by executing a discharge of standard security which is prepared by the solicitors instructed to act for the bank and sometimes is contained on the reverse of the standard security deed itself. The standard security and the discharge will be placed with the other title deeds relating to the property, all of which are returned to the customer.

Remaining with the situation in Scotland, if the standard security has been granted by a company and is therefore disclosed on the company's Register of Charges with the Registrar of Companies, it is usual for the Registrar to be notified that the charge has been discharged or satisfied. Similarly, when a bond and floating charge is no longer required by a bank, it is usual for the Registrar of Companies to be notified by means of a Memorandum of Satisfaction which is completed by the company and, in the case of a bond and floating charge, certified by the bank and then lodged with the Registrar. There is no time limit for lodging a memorandum of satisfaction after it has been completed. The situation in England and Wales where the bank holds a legal charge is that the bank will effect its release by executing a discharge. This will be actioned through the bank's legal representatives.

Question   **10**

Go to question section starting on page 243

Check with the answer at the back of the book.

Review

Now consider the main learning points which were introduced in this chapter.

Go through them and tick each one when you are happy that you fully understand each point.

Then check back to the objectives at the beginning of the chapter and match them to the learning points.

Reread any section you are unsure of before moving on.

A bank takes security to guard against any unforeseen circumstances which may affect the customer's ability to repay an advance.

☐

Direct security is security granted by the borrower for their own obligations whereas third party security is provided by someone other than the borrower but is available for the borrower's obligations.

☐

The attributes of a good security are: simplicity of title, stability of value and realisability.

☐

A guarantee is an undertaking by one party to answer for the debt or default of another person.

☐

The arrangements for taking security over land and buildings differs between Scotland and England/Wales. However, both processes require the use of lawyers and the appropriate registration of the security.

☐

A life policy is a contract to pay a cash sum on the occurrence of a specified event or the elapse of an agreed period of time in return for the payment of a premium. To take it as security requires the completion of an assignation.

☐

To take security over marketable securities requires the completion of a letter of pledge and the transfer of the securities into the bank's nominee company.

☐

A bond and floating charge can only be granted by a company and the charge does not attach to any particular company asset.

☐

A customer granting security of a cash deposit will sign a letter of pledge.

☐

Often all that is required to discharge security is for the bank to confirm in writing that it is no longer looking to the item of security for the obligations of the customer.

☐

Key words in this chapter are given below. There is space to write your own revision notes and to add any other words or phrases that you want to remember.

direct security

third party security

simplicity of title

stability of value

realisability

undue influence

standard security/Legal Charge

postponed securities

ranking agreement

endowment policy

term assurance

whole life policy

life assured

nominal value

market value

letter of pledge

memorandum of satisfaction

Multiple choice questions   **8**

Try these self-test questions to assess your understanding of what you have read in this chapter.
The answers are at the back of the book.

1   The main type of security taken in respect of a residential mortgage advance is which one of the following?

    A   mortgage indemnity guarantee

    B   assignation of life policies

    C   bond and floating charge

    D   standard security/legal Charge

2   Security granted by the borrower for his own obligations is known as which one of the following?

    A   direct security

    B   indirect security

    C   primary security

    D   personal covenant

3   Which one of the following is not an attribute of good security for a debt?

    A   simplicity of title

    B   stability of value

    C   tangibility

    D   realisability

Multiple choice questions   **8**

4 Which one of the following types of security provides the bank with no security rights or asset with which it can deal?

A   stocks and shares

B   personal guarantee

C   residential home

D   bond and floating charge

5 Which one of the following is most likely to affect a bank's right to realise its security in the form of a residential property?

A   where the property is subject to an interest only loan with a life policy assigned to the lender

B   where the borrower is using the property for business purposes

C   where the property has been let out to a tenant

D   where the borrower has vacated the property

6 In order to ensure that a guarantor completely understands the implications of the personal guarantee, which one of the following actions should the bank take?

A   advise the guarantor to discuss the matter with the principal borrower

B   advise the guarantor to seek independent financial advice

C   advise the guarantor to seek independent legal advice

D   explain all provisions of the guarantee if asked to do so

Multiple choice questions   **8**

7   In order to make the insurance company aware of an assignation, which one of the following steps is taken by the bank?

A   the bank intimates assignation to the insurance company

B   the bank accepts a pledge by the borrower

C   the bank registers the assignation at the Land Registry

D   the bank registers the assignation at the Register of Sasines

8   The person who will be paid the proceeds of a life assurance policy is called the:

A   Recipient

B   Beneficiary

C   Payee

D   Legatee

9   Within what period of time must a charge granted by a company be registered with the Registrar of Companies?

A   seven days

B   fourteen days

C   twenty-one days

D   twenty-eight days

Multiple choice questions   **8**

10 The market value of shares is an indication of which one of the following?

A   the actual value of the company's assets

B   the future financial prospects of the company

C   the demand of investors for the shares

D   the book value of the company

11 When taking security by way of company shares, the shares are transferred to which one of the following?

A   a nominee company

B   the bank

C   the bank's solicitors

D   the Registrar of Companies

12 Which one of the following possesses all of the attributes of a good security?

A   a residential property

B   a cash deposit

C   listed shares

D   bond and floating charge

Questions

Question 1

1   The mother of your customer, Karl Williams, calls into the office as she is concerned that Karl has issued a cheque, but there are not enough funds in the account to cover it. She explains that she will pay enough into the account to pay the cheque. How would you respond?

2   Can you describe any circumstances where it might be in the interests of the bank to divulge information about the affairs of one of its customers?

3   Is a banker a mere custodian of the customer's money?

4   What duties does a customer have to his or her bank?

5   What do you understand by the Banking Conduct of Business Sourcebook?

Question 2

1   What is the difference between savings and investment?

2   In what ways does an interest paying current account differ from a high interest cheque account?

3   What is a standing order? Is it the same as a direct debit?

4   What is a contract note?

5   Does an executor require to be named in the will of a deceased person?

6   What do you understand by portfolio management?

Question 3

1   What is meant by joint and several liability?

2   Your customer Graeme Wilson calls into the bank to advise that he and his wife have purchased a shop and they would like to open a business account. How should the cheque book be styled and what other advice can you give to Mr Wilson?

3   What do you understand by the term "limited liability"?

4   A company has debts of £50,000 when it ceased trading. The company has three directors. What is the extent of each director's liability for the

debts of the company, assuming that no personal guarantees have been signed?

5   What is the rule in Clayton's case?

6   What is the danger to a bank in lending money to a curling club?

7   What are a company's articles?

Question 4

1   What is the correct procedure for a bank paying the balance standing to the credit of an account in the name of a deceased customer?

2   What is the effect of lodging an arrestment/garnishee order in the hands of a bank?

3   What information can a bank obtain about customers by examining their bank accounts?

4   One of your customers maintains a current account on which there is presently a creditor balance of £357. The account has just returned to credit after a period of six months when it was overdrawn without the prior approval of the bank and you now wish the bank account to be closed. How should you proceed?

5   What are the benefits of conducting an annual review with a customer?

6   What is the rule in Clayton's case?

7   What should a banker bear in mind before dishonouring a cheque drawn by a business customer?

8   You note from the local newspaper that your customer James McGregor died two days ago. He maintained a current account with a creditor balance of £2,500. A cheque for £50 has today been presented for payment. What is the correct procedure to be followed by the bank?

9   What is the difference between testate and intestate succession?

Question 5

1   What is the main provision of the Cheques Act 1992?

2   One of your customers who has a local shop presents her bank statement to you and asks why, given that her account has remained in credit for

the year, she has been charged interest. How would you explain this situation to her?

3 You are advised that one of your customers has died during the night. The same morning you receive through the clearing a cheque issued by the customer dated three days ago, a cheque drawn by Avis Electronics Limited and signed by your customer who is a director of the company and a cheque signed by your customer as a partner of the firm of Evergreen Electronics. How would you deal with the cheques?

4 Can a cheque be written out in pencil? If not, why not?

5 What are uncleared funds?

6 You receive a telephone call from one of your customers asking you to stop payment of a cheque. You note that the cheque was received by you in the clearing this morning. How do you react?

7 One of your customers, Peter Hyde, works in the local supermarket and has his salary lodged to his account monthly. You notice that the present balance on his account is £300,403 and on further investigation you note that a cheque for £300,000 was lodged to the account three days ago. A cheque for £275,000 payable to "J Smith" is in the morning clearing. What do you do?

Question 6

1 What is the difference between a credit card and a charge card?

2 Explain how a credit card can provide the holder with interest-free credit.

3 Explain briefly the procedure for buying goods and services at point of sale with a debit card.

4 What is CHAPS?

Question 7

1 What is an arrangement fee? When and why should such a fee be charged?

2 Should a bank always insist on having security when lending to a customer?

3 Why is a cash flow forecast useful to a banker?

4   State briefly the points that should be considered when analysing a lending proposition assuming that you are satisfied about the integrity and means of the proposed borrower.

5   What is the significance of a customer having a land telephone line when credit scoring a loan application?

6   What is the difference between a capital release loan and a bridging loan?

7   What information can a banker obtain about a personal customer from their bank account?

Question 8

In each of the following examples identify the proposer, the beneficiary, the life assured and the type of assurance that would be taken out.

Example 1

James Robertson wishes to provide for his retirement and is prepared to pay premiums to a life assurance company so that when he is sixty years old he will receive £100,000. He is married to Jean and has two sons, William and John.

Proposer:

Beneficiary:

Life Assured:

Type of Assurance:

Example 2:

Graeme Jackson wishes his son Colin to get off to a good start when he graduates from University and is willing to ensure that Colin receives the sum of £45,000 on his twenty first birthday.

Proposer

Beneficiary

Life Assured

Type of Assurance

Example 3:

Graeme Jackson has a young daughter, Janice. He wishes to make provisions so that when she gets married he will be able to pay for a large wedding reception. He reckons that she will not get married until she is at least twenty years old.

Proposer

Beneficiary

Life Assured

Type of Assurance

Example 4:

William Ross wishes to make sure that his wife, Helen, will be provided for in the event of his dying while he is still earning a salary.

Proposer

Beneficiary

Life Assured

Type of Assurance

Example 5:

Robert Jones is concerned that his young wife, Fiona, will not be able to support herself after he dies.

Proposer

Beneficiary

Life Assured

Type of Assurance

Question 9

1   What are the advantages to a bank in surrendering a life policy?

2   A bank grants a mortgage to James and Fiona Roundel. James works as an estate agent and Fiona stays at home to look after their two children. The bank will be granted security over the house to be purchased and

the value of the house is considerably more than the amount of the mortgage. The couple have no other obligations to the bank. In these circumstances, what are the advantages, if any, in the bank taking an assignation of a life policy?

Question 10

1   What attributes of a good security can be found in a guarantee?

2   What is the difference between direct security and third party security?

3   What underlying factors should a banker consider when offered a pledge of marketable securities?

4   What is endowment assurance?

5   How is a pledge of marketable securities discharged?

Answers to Question

Question 1

1 The bank has a duty of confidentiality to all its customers and Mrs Williams's request should be politely declined, but there is nothing to prevent her from making a lodgement to her son's account if she so desires.

2 If a bank wishes to take recovery action against one of its customers, it is often necessary to instruct solicitors or recovery agents who have to be advised of the amount of the customer's debt and any other information about the customer the bank may have. Similarly, if the bank is to be granted security by the customer and it is necessary to instruct solicitors to act on the bank's behalf, details of the borrowing facilities that are to be afforded to the customer will have to be divulged. There are several other instances.

3 The banker is more than a mere custodian of his or her customers' money. This term implies that the customer will receive the same notes and coins as were originally paid in whereas when money is paid in, it is used by the bank for the purposes of its business and the bank undertakes an obligation to repay an equivalent amount.

4 A customer must make suitable provision for any cheques they issue and must draw their cheques in regular form and exercise due care not to facilitate forgery or conversion.

5 BCOBS is a mandatory Code which is regulated by the FCA. It sets out the standards that retail banks must employ when dealing with their customers.

Question 2

1 Savings is retained income – surplus funds that have been set aside for a purpose – whereas investment is when the set-aside funds are expected to grow or to provide income. The return on savings comes from interest, the returns from investments can be dividend and/or capital growth. Savings are risk free, but the value of investments can fall as well as rise.

2 A high interest cheque account normally pays a higher rate of interest than an interest paying current account, but there may be restrictions on

the number of transactions that can be made on a high interest cheque account and a minimum amount for which a cheque may be drawn, whereas customers have unrestricted access to funds in an interest paying current account and will not normally incur any charges unless the account becomes overdrawn. There is normally a minimum creditor balance that must be maintained in a high interest cheque account, otherwise normal current account conditions will apply.

3   A standing order is a signed authority given by a customer to a bank, instructing the bank to make regular payments from the customer's account to a specified party (or to another account in name of the customer) at stated times for a stated period or until further notice.

Direct debits are similar to standing orders in a number of ways, but the important difference is that, rather than the customer's bank remitting the payment to the beneficiary's bank, the beneficiary instigates the debit and advises the customer's bank of the amount involved. Direct debits are becoming more popular than standing orders.

4   A contract note is issued by a stockbroker and contains details of securities purchased or sold on behalf of the customer. Details of the type and number of securities bought or sold, the price, the commissions payable and the date on which the transaction will settle appear on the contract note and then the relative sums will be paid over.

5   It is common for an executor to be appointed in terms of the will of a deceased person, but if the will fails to nominate an executor or the deceased died intestate (without making a will) an executor can be appointed by the court on application.

6   This service is normally offered through a specialist subsidiary company of a bank and involves the managing of shares held by a customer. This can involve the organisation buying or selling shares on behalf of the customer, having first of all agreed an investment strategy.

Question 3

1   All parties liable for an obligation are each liable for the full amount of the obligation; for example, if a bank account is £10,000 overdrawn and there are two parties to the account, if the parties are jointly and severally liable, the bank could look to either party for the full £10,000.

2   If Mr Wilson and his wife have purchased the shop and intend operating the shop together then, in the eyes of the law, they are in partnership.

It is not essential for Mr and Mrs Wilson to enter into a contract of co-partnery, but it will be necessary for a partnership mandate to be provided to the bank. The customers should also advise the bank of the name of the firm and the cheque book should also disclose the firm's name in order to comply with the Business Names Act.

3 Limited liability describes the liability of a shareholder of a company for the debts of the company. A shareholder is only personally liable for the debts of the company in which he or she holds shares to the extent of any money still to be paid to the company in respect of the shares.

4 Under normal circumstances, directors of a company are not personally liable for the company's debts. If the directors are also shareholders, they will be liable for the company's debts only to the extent of sums due but not paid in respect of the shares issued to them

5 The rule in Clayton's case is that the earliest debit to a running account is repaid by the first lodgement. This is an important principle for bankers, especially in the event of the bank wishing to preserve the liability of a party (or their estate) to an overdrawn bank account.

6 The main danger to a bank in lending to the curling club, or any other type of unincorporated body, is that the club has no legal personality and so it can only raise an action or be sued in the name of the members. In practice it will be difficult for the banker to establish that individual members are personally liable for repayment of the overdraft in the event of club funds not being sufficient.

7 The articles are the rules governing the internal relationships within a company.

Question 4

1 The bank should make payment to the personal representatives of the deceased who must exhibit the relevant authorising documentation. This documentation should include details of the deceased's estate. Before making payment, the bank should note these details, including the balance of the bank account and any other assets held by the bank.

2 The lodging of an arrestment/garnishee order in the hands of a bank would prevent the person named in the arrestment/garnishee order having access to the credit funds in their account.

3 If the customer's salary is mandated to the bank, the name of the customer's employer and the current level of their salary will be known.

By taking a note of the standing orders and direct debits on the account, the banker will be aware of the customer's regular commitments. The names of the payees of cheques and/or card payments issued by the customer will let the banker see how the customer is spending their money. This is particularly useful in the case of business customers.

4   It is necessary for the bank to give the customer reasonable notice of its intention to close the account. There is a danger in the bank remitting the outstanding creditor balance to the customer as there could be outstanding cheques/debits and the banker would be on dangerous ground in refusing to pay such cheques as the customer did have funds to meet the cheques when they were issued. The correct procedure would be for the bank to advise the customer that it is the bank's wish that the account be closed. The customer should be requested not to issue any further cheques and to draw a cheque for the outstanding balance on the account.

5   The banker can see whether or not the facilities provided to the customer are still required at the current level. It will also be possible to compare the transactions on the account with the projections and the cash flow forecast provided by the customer at the time the facilities were originally requested or at the last review. It is also possible to check that the customer is not misusing the facilities, although this should be apparent from regular monitoring of the account.

6   The basic rule is that the first lodgement to an account is withdrawn by the first withdrawal from the account and the first debit to an account is repaid by the first lodgement. For example, if a firm's current account is overdrawn to the extent of £50,000 and the bank is advised that one of the partners of the firm has resigned, the bank must stop operations on the firm's account if it wishes to preserve the retiring partner's liability to the bank. If operations are not stopped, once the sum of £50,000 has been lodged to the account, even if, as a result of further debits to the account the overdraft remains at £50,000, the £50,000 liability of the retiring partner will have been repaid and the £50,000 then outstanding will be a "different" £50,000 from the sum outstanding at the time the bank was made aware of the resignation.

7   First of all, as it is one of the bank's primary duties to its customers to pay cheques issued by them provided that there are sufficient funds to meet the cheque, the banker should take all reasonable steps to make

sure that there are definitely insufficient funds to enable the cheque to be paid. Before returning the cheque the banker should consider what effect dishonouring the cheque will have on the customer's business and its relationship with its suppliers and/or customers, especially if the bank is making facilities available to the customer, repayment of which depends largely on the ongoing business activities. In addition, careful consideration must be given to cheques in respect of the rental of the customer's business premises or for the purchase or rental of essential business equipment.

8   The authority of a banker to pay cheques drawn by a customer ceases as soon as the banker receives notice of the customer's death, therefore the cheque should be returned unpaid with answer "Drawer Deceased". Payment of the outstanding creditor balance will be paid by the bank to the personal representatives of the customer, or, if the estate is small, the bank may be willing to make payment to the personal representatives against a suitable discharge and guarantee.

9   If someone dies leaving a will they are said to have died testate, but if they die without leaving a will they have died intestate.

Question 5

1   The Cheques Act 1992 provided for crossed cheques and certain other types of cheque to be non-transferable which means that they cannot be accepted for credit of any account other than an account in name of the named payee of the cheque.

2   It should be explained to the customer that cheques lodged for payment are not regarded by the bank as being cleared funds until sufficient time has elapsed for the bank to be certain that the cheques have been paid by the bank on which they have been drawn. If the customer has drawn cheques against funds that are not regarded as cleared funds, the customer will be liable for deferment interest.

3   Notice of a customer's death terminates a banker's authority to pay the customer's cheques. The cheque drawn by the customer on their own account should therefore be returned unpaid with the answer "Drawer Deceased". Cheques issued by a company and signed by a director are not affected by the death of the director. Similarly, cheques issued by a firm and signed by a partner can still be paid notwithstanding the death of the partner. The cheques drawn by Avis Electronics Limited and the

firm of Evergreen Electronics can therefore be paid, provided of course there are no other reasons why the cheques should not be paid, such as insufficient funds.

4   It is not unlawful for cheques to be written in pencil, but banks actively discourage such a practice as such cheques can easily be altered.

5   When a customer of a bank lodges to their account a cheque drawn on another bank or another branch of the same bank, the amount involved is credited to the customer's account immediately. When the account is credited, however, neither the customer nor the bank know whether or not the cheque will be paid when it is presented through the clearing system to the bank on which it is drawn. It will take several days for the cheque to "clear" and during this time the amount credited to the bank account is regarded as uncleared funds or uncleared effects. Often customers will not be permitted to draw their own cheques against uncleared funds. In the event of their being permitted to do so, they can be charged deferment interest if, as result of the issue of cheques, the cleared balance on the account is overdrawn.

6   The cheque can be returned unpaid as the banker has until close of business on the day that a cheque is presented through the clearing system to decide whether or not the cheque will be paid. It would be prudent of course to confirm the serial number of the cheque and to arrange to have the stop request confirmed in writing as soon as possible, preferably before the cheque was returned.

7   When collecting cheques for one of its customers, the bank is exposed to the danger that it may collect a cheque to which its customer has no title. The bank is protected by statute in such circumstances and will not be liable to the true owner of the cheque provided the bank acts in good faith and without negligence and acts for a customer.

Peter Hyde is clearly a customer, but the bank may be regarded as being negligent if it is not put on enquiry by what are clearly transactions on an account which are incompatible with the circumstances of the customer. There may of course be a legitimate reason behind the lodgement of such a large cheque and the issue of a similarly large cheque, but the banker must make enquiries to be satisfied that this is the case. There will also be considerations to be made to the anti-money laundering regulations regarding this lodgement which should have been discussed with the customer.

Question 6

1   The main difference between a credit card and a charge card is that, while with a credit card the customer has the option of paying off only part of the sums due in terms of the monthly statement (normally a minimum of 3 - 5%), in the case of a charge card the whole outstanding balance must be cleared monthly.

2   Provided a cardholder pays off the whole balance due to the credit card company, they will not be charged any interest. Statements are issued monthly by the credit card company and do not require to be settled until 21 days after the date of the statement. It could be that a cardholder will make a purchase using their card, and by the time the transaction has been advised to the credit card company the cut-off date for the next statement may just have passed. From that date it could therefore be another 31 days before the purchases appear on the cardholder's statement and 21 days after that before the cardholder is required to make payment. It can be possible for the customer to enjoy interest-free credit for a period of up to 56 days, sometimes even longer.

3   The purchaser will present the debit card to the retailer who either swipes the card or inserts it into a card reader. The customer will input their PIN and thus the transaction is completed. The customer's account will be debited for the transaction and the retailer's account will be credited.

4   Clearing House Automated Payment System, which sends same day high-value payments from one member bank to another.

Question 7

1   An arrangement fee is often charged by a bank to cover the costs in arranging the facility. There are also costs involved in meeting with the customer to discuss the facility and in the lending proposition being analysed, sanctioned and having the appropriate documentation prepared.

2   Any decision by a bank to lend money to one of its customers will depend on its view of the customer's present and future ability to repay the advance from the customer's own resources. Although consideration will be given to the need for security and in many cases security will be desirable, it should not be regarded as an alternative source of

repayment; rather it is put in place to provide a safety net against some unforeseen future events.

3   A cash flow forecast is useful as it can let the banker see that the correct level of advance has been requested and will also demonstrate how the advance will be repaid and the timing of receipts and outflows of cash from the business.

4   The main points that should be considered are:

- the character, means, financial acumen and ability of the borrower

- the soundness of the lending proposition

- the security available

- the viability of the proposed repayment arrangements, including how realistic or conservative are the projections and forecasts provided by the borrower

- the interest, fees and charges that will be paid to the bank to determine whether the lending proposition is profitable for the bank.

5   There are two areas of importance:

- if the customer has had difficulty making payment to the line provider, this will be reflected in some adverse credit information on the customer

- if the loan is sanctioned and falls into arrears, having the customer's phone number will make it easier for the bank to make contact.

6   A capital or equity release loan is a loan that is made available to house owners who have a reversion on their property which means that the value of the borrower's property is significantly in excess of the outstanding house purchase loan. A borrower can borrow a percentage of the reversion or equity on the property by means of an equity release loan. If the bank granting the loan is not the same bank as granted the house purchase loan, it will be necessary for the customer to grant a second charge over the property in favour of the bank.

A bridging loan is made available usually in connection with house purchases and bridges the gap between the time when a customer has to make payment for a property that they have purchased and the time when the sale proceeds for the property that has just been sold are received.

7   The banker will have a good idea of the customer's level of salary and the name of the customer's employer, particularly if the salary is mandated to the bank. The standing orders, direct debits and regular payments made from the account will reveal the customer's spending pattern and regular commitments. The banker will also be able to see the name of the customer's mortgage lender and have a rough idea of the amount of house purchase loan that has been made available.

Question 8

Example 1:

Proposer	James Robertson
Beneficiary	James Robertson
Life Assured	James Robertson
Type of Assurance	Endowment

Example 2:

Proposer	Graeme Jackson
Beneficiary	Colin Jackson
Life Assured	Colin Jackson
Type of Assurance	Endowment

Example 3:

Proposer	Graeme Jackson
Beneficiary	Graeme Jackson
Life Assured	Probably Janice Jackson but it could also be Graeme Jackson
Type of Assurance	Endowment

Example 4:

Proposer	William Ross
Beneficiary	Helen Ross
Life Assured	William Ross
Type of Assurance	Term assurance

Example 5:

Proposer	Robert Jones
Beneficiary	Fiona Jones
Life Assured	Robert Jones
Type of Assurance	Whole life

Question 9

1   A bank can surrender a life policy at any time in the event of the customer being unable to meet their obligations and can therefore obtain funds immediately rather than having to hold the policy and maintain the premiums until maturity. This would also result in there being higher interest payments debited to the customer's account. However, the surrender value will often be considerably less than the maturity value.

2   Notwithstanding the value of the property, it is advisable from the point of view of both the bank and the customers for the bank to be granted an assignation of life cover on the joint lives of James and Fiona. Without an assignation of life cover, in the event of James dying, the only way that the bank can be repaid would be for the house to be sold. This is a course of action that both the bank and the customers would wish to avoid, especially if it entailed the bank entering into possession of the property.

Question 10

1   The attributes of a good security are:

- simplicity of title
- stability of value
- realisability.

A guarantee can be constituted easily and cheaply, therefore it is fair to say that the attribute simplicity of title is present in a guarantee. It is of course the case that a guarantee will normally be for a certain sum, but this should not be confused with stability of value as the value of the guarantee is dependent on the means of the guarantor, particularly in the case of unsupported guarantees. With regard to realisability, it is often said that a guarantee is the easiest item of security to constitute but often the most difficult to realise. Unless the guarantor is willing and able to settle their guarantee obligation or agree repayment arrangements, it may prove necessary for the bank to take recovery action against the guarantor and to take steps to realise any supporting security.

2   Direct security is security granted by the borrower for their own obligations, whereas third party security is provided by someone other than the borrower but is available for the obligations of the borrower.

3   The banker should consider whether or not the current value of the shares provide an adequate margin to cater for fluctuations in the price(s) of the shares. It is worth considering whether or not the shares offered represent a wide and balanced portfolio of shares or if they are predominantly in one or two companies.

4   In return for the payment of premiums, endowment assurance will entitle the policyholder to be paid an assured sum on survival for a stated period or on earlier death. The policyholder will also be entitled to a share in the profits made by the life assurance company.

5   The banker will advise the person who has pledged the shares that the letter of pledge has been cancelled or will return the cancelled letter of pledge to the customer. Arrangements will also be made to transfer the shares pledged from the name of the bank's nominee company back into the name of the true owner of the shares.

Answers to Multiple choice questions

Multiple choice questions **1**

1	B	6	B
2	C	7	C
3	A	8	D
4	D		
5	C		

Multiple choice questions **2**

1	C	8	C
2	D	9	D
3	A	10	A
4	C	11	C
5	A	12	C
6	D	13	C
7	C		

Multiple choice questions **3**

1	B	9	D
2	D	10	B
3	D	11	D
4	B	12	A
5	A	13	D
6	C	14	C
7	D	15	B
8	C		

Multiple choice questions **4**

1	B	6	D
2	C	7	C
3	B	8	D
4	B	9	A
5	C		

Multiple choice questions **5**

1	C	6	B
2	B	7	D
3	B	8	C
4	C		
5	C		

Multiple choice questions **6**

1	D
2	B
3	B
4	D

Multiple choice questions **7**

1	C	6	D
2	B	7	B
3	C		
4	C		
5	C		

Multiple choice questions **8**

1	D	7	A
2	A	8	B
3	C	9	C
4	B	10	C
5	C	11	A
6	C	12	B

Glossary

Articles of Association	Document setting out the internal rules of a limited company.
Arrangement fee	A charge made by a bank to cover the costs involved in arranging and agreeing a loan.
Arrestment /Garnishee Order	An order served on a debtor compelling it to holds funds held to the credit of a third party named in the order.
Automatic Call Distribution (ACD)	A routing system for calls once they arrive at a telephone centre.
Automated telephone service	The service offered to a customer when they telephone an organisation and are greeted by a recorded message offering them some service options.
Bank giro credit	A credit transfer form used by customers for making non-automated payments to accounts domiciled at a branch or bank other than the branch where the customer's account is held.
Banking Conduct of Business Sourcebook	Compulsory rules and guidelines that regulate retail banking
Basic bank account	An account which offers the customer a basic range of money transmission facilities. A plastic card will be provided to facilitate withdrawals of cash at an ATM. Automated payments can also be credited to the account.
Bond and floating charge	A security that can only be granted by a company. The charge does not attach to any particular company asset.

Bridging loan	A (usually) short term loan used when a customer has to make a large purchase before the receipt of funds for a large scale purchase. Normally associated with house purchase transactions when the customer is required to pay for their new home before receiving the sale proceeds from their old home.
Call up notice	A notice issued by a bank after the default notice; only issued when the bank is holding security. Its purpose is to call up the security, not the debt.
Canons of lending	The principles of credit assessment.
Cash flow projection	A statement showing how much cash the customer has presently, what their projected income and expenditure will be and therefore how much cash they will have at the end of the period.
Certificate of Incorporation	Certificate issued by the Registrar of Companies when a new limited company is founded and complies with the regulations as set out in the Companies Acts.
CHAPS	Clearing House Automated Payment System – an electronic credit transfer system for sending same day value sterling payments from one member bank to another.
Clayton's case	The rule whereby the first credit to an account eliminates the oldest debit.
Collections department	A specialist department in a bank which seeks to obtain repayment from certain irregular accounts. The aim of the collections process is to bring the account

back on to a regular footing, whilst preserving the long term relationship with the customer.

Countermanding	The placing of a stop payment instruction from a customer.
Covenant	Conditions imposed on a customer when obtaining a loan; usually set out in a loan agreement.
Credit scoring	A statistical means of assessing the probability of repayment of credit for an individual or small business who supplies specific data when applying for credit.
Crystallisation of a floating charge	When a bank appoints a receiver the bond and floating charge attaches specifically to the assets owned by the company at the time.
Current account	Sometimes referred to as money transmission accounts, as they are used to deposit and withdraw funds, usually on a frequent basis. Operated usually by a plastic card and cheque book. Will normally pay some amount of interest on credit balances, debit interest is charged on overdrawn balances.
Customer profiling	An activity where the bank finds out as much information as possible about a customer's circumstances, their background and aspirations. This information is then used to match the most suitable products and services to the customer.
Default notice	A notice served by a bank to a defaulting customer, explaining to the customer that they have breached the terms of their credit agreement.

Deferment interest	Interest charged to a customer when they have drawn against uncleared effects.
Direct debit	A signed authority from a customer to the bank, authorising them to accept payments from a named beneficiary who instigates the debit and advises the bank of the amount involved.
Direct security	Security granted by a borrower against their own debts.
Due diligence	The steps taken to identify relevant information about either a new customer or a borrowing customer.
Equity release loan	A lower cost loan of up to a certain percentage of the equity in a customer's home provided that the bank is granted security over the property.
Executor	Someone who is appointed to ensure that the wishes of a deceased person, as set out in his or her will, are carried out.
Faster Payments	A system used to make immediate payment up to £100,000 thus avoiding the use of the clearing system
Financial intermediation	The role played by banks whereby they act as a conduit between those in the economy with surplus funds and those with insufficient funds
Guarantee	An undertaking by one party to answer for the debt or default of another person.
Hard core borrowing	The situation where an overdraft does not swing into credit. The hard core element is the amount of the lowest overdrawn balance.
High interest cheque account	An account that allows the customer to have instant access to their funds but with

restrictions on the number of cheques that may be issued in a given period and cheques may require to be for not less than a stated amount.

Home reversion plan | Where all or part of a property is sold to a financial services firm and the original owner becomes a tenant.

House cheque | A cheque that has been drawn on the same branch of the bank as the one where the payee is making the lodgement.

Individual Savings Account (ISA) | A tax-free savings account, offered to UK residents aged 18 and over (aged 16 and over for a cash ISA). There are maximum amounts which may be deposited in any one tax year. It is possible to have cash and equity ISAs.

Interest only mortgage | A mortgage which has no repayments of any capital at all during the life of the loan. The payment made by the customer to the lender only covers the interest accruing on the loan.

Intestate | Where a person has died without leaving a will.

Investment account | A higher interest paying account which has a minimum qualifying balance, a period of notice of withdrawal and a restriction on the number of withdrawals.

Joint and several liability | An arrangement between a bank and its customers where there are more than two parties to the agreement. The arrangement is that each party will be held liable for the full amount of the debt.

Legal Charge | The document used in England and Wales to take security over land and property

Life assurance	A contract that provides payment on the death of an insured but may also include payment on a specified date should the insured survive until that date.
Lifetime mortgage	A product that allows older customers to borrow up to 25% of the value of a mortgage-free property
Limited company	A business structure where the business has a separate legal personality from its owners.
Money laundering	The process by which the proceeds of crime are converted into assets that seem to have a legitimate origin.
Money transmission	The transfer of money from one party to another, normally from the receiver of goods and services to the supplier of goods and services.
Negotiable instrument	A document that can be negotiated for value and may be passed from one party to another.
Nominee company	A company set up specifically to hold shares pledged to the bank.
Overdraft	A negative balance on a current account. It may be authorised or unauthorised.
Partnership	A business structure where two or more people are trading together in an attempt to make profits.
Part 4A Permission	The authority granted from the Regulator to a bank which allows them to accept deposits from the public
Personal loan	A loan granted to a personal customer for a fixed period of time to assist with the purchase of a range of items.

Personal representatives	These persons involved in the collection and distribution of a deceased person's estate
Recoveries department	A specialist department of a bank which deals with irregular accounts after the collections department have concluded their activities with these customers and the account is still irregular. The aim of a recoveries department is to collect the debt whilst severing the relationship with the customer.
Repayment mortgage	A mortgage that requires the borrower to repay part of the capital borrowed and an interest payment charged on that capital every time an instalment is made. The balance of the account should be zero by the end of the loan period.
Scorecard	The set of points used when credit scoring an application.
Second mortgage	A loan secured on a property obtained from a different lender
Shareholder	The owner (or part owner) of a limited company who has invested money in the company by purchasing shares.
Sole trader	A person carrying on business on their own.
Stale cheque	A cheque that has been in circulation for what is considered an unreasonably long time. The practice is for banks to regard cheques more that six months old as being stale.
Standard security	The only document that can be used to secure debt against heritable property in Scotland.

Standing order	A signed authority given by a customer to a bank instructing the bank to make regular payments from the customer's account to a specified party at stated times for a stated period or until further notice.
Term loan	A loan usually granted to business customers to assist them in buying assets such as plant and machinery where the cost involved would make it inappropriate for the borrowing to be added to the overdraft facility which should be used for working capital purposes.
Testate	Where a person has died leaving a will.
Third party payment	A payment made by a customer, through their financial services provider, to another person.
Third party security	Security provided by someone other than the borrower but that is available for the borrower's obligations.
Treating Customers Fairly	The initiative designed to ensure the equitable treatment of customers by UK banks.
Truncation	The removal of the obligation to send cheques back to the relevant branch of the paying bank. When a cheque is truncated it is retained at some point in the clearing process.
Trustee	A person who has been trusted to hold and administer property or assets for the benefit of others.
Uncleared effects	The proceeds of cheques that have not yet been paid by the drawee bank; in other words, the cheques are still in the clearing system.

Undue influence

The situation where a stronger party, as a matter of law or provable from prevailing circumstances, induces a weaker party to enter into a contract where he or she would not otherwise do so.

Index

A

B

C